# BEYOND THE RIVER'S GATE

Stewart Bitkoff, Ed.D.

Abandoned Ladder

Copyright © 2014 by Stewart Bitkoff

goldpath@ptd.net

Except as permitted under U.S. Copyright Law, no part of this book may be reprinted, reproduced, transmitted, or utilized in any form by any electronic, mechanical, or other means, now known or hereafter invented, including photocopying, microfilming, and recording, or in any information storage or retrieval system, without written permission from the publisher.

Printed in the United States of America

ISBN-13: 978-0-9915775-0-7
ISBN-10: 0991577507

10 9 8 7 6 5 4 3 2 1

This book is for travelers everywhere:
Fighting illness, suffering
And straining to reach Higher.

May a ladder of Light
Be extended, lifting you up,
Far beyond tears, pain and sadness.

*-SB*

*Religion may be compared*
*To a great river that feeds the land.*
*The river winds its way as a mighty force*
*And smaller tributaries are formed*
*To serve the distant regions.*
*Some travelers are satisfied*
*To drink of the smaller stream*
*And forget they must travel*
*The river to its Source.*

*Beyond the river's gate,*
*The Ocean is waiting.*

*-SB*

## Note to Reader

**First, I'd like to present a few thoughts on why I was inspired to write this book and share the messages contained here with a wider audience.**

In my life, I often behaved as if godliness was next to idleness. Most often I sought time away by myself to contemplate how spiritual I was. I truly believed salvation was to be found, away from others, meditating upon profound thoughts.

And when I traveled a little further, I realized 'contemplating my navel' was the antithesis of what the Path was about. As Saadi taught, so many years ago, "The Path is in human service. It is none other than this." This is still true today.

When a hand is extended to help another, the human soul reaches toward the heavens. Service that is free of personal interest is one of the highest forms of human existence.

And so I present this work as a form of service to my fellow humans here on Earth, most of who are spiritual travelers, just like me.

**And now, a few notes about the format of this book. In literary works readers have come to expect material to follow a basic, familiar structure. Usually this format includes the following:**

- The writing has a clear beginning, middle and end. The use of chapters allows similar material to be grouped together
- There is a central theme or set of ideas that is discernible, flowing and developing through sections

and chapters.
- Through the writer's expertise, the reader is brought to reach their own conclusions rather than being told what the conclusion should be.

Spiritual writing often does not adhere to the structure described above. This type of writing is designed to impact on an inner level, using a scatter approach and a different set of underlying principles. It works on a conscious, subconscious and spiritual level. Sometimes the synergy of understanding takes months or years to achieve.

<u>Beyond the River's Gate</u> is divided into two sections. Part I is a collection of 99 question and answers that cover a range of spiritual topics. Part II presents stories, verses, sayings and observations that enrich this material.

Collectively, this writing explores basic concerns that people have about the spiritual journey and its connection to world problems. Many of us have had a religious upbringing but we may lack an inner connection to what we learned, and wonder what to do with this early learning in our day-to-day lives.

Further, this material focuses on making that inner spiritual connection; most importantly that connection is the point at which religion and spirituality meet. For millennia, the wise have claimed on an inner level, all the religions are one. By shining a Light on spiritual learning and mystery traditions which have long been hidden, it is intended that the information presented will stimulate and push the reader further to seek their own questions and answers.

So here our questioning, rational mind is represented by each question and higher consciousness or spirit is its answer. While these questions may appear at times random and unconnected, this is in fact the way higher consciousness or spiritual learning takes place. At times our thoughts and questions are all over the place. Yet another part of our awareness, which is deeply hidden, works to integrate and provide balance and direction.

Most often, the answer to questions is openly stated and provides a grounding framework for the reader. You do not have to wonder what the author is trying to say. This is done so that you might react and learn. The ability to observe our reactions and master our responses is one of the goals of the spiritual journey.

In this regard may this writing be of service and may your journey be filled with Light.

Finally, as you travel through these pages, may you take this information and reach toward the ultimate question and answer: understanding who you are and creating your own, individual destiny.

-SB

# Contents

Note to Reader . . . . . . . . . . . . . . . . . . . .  vii

**Contents**  x

## I  Questions & Answers  1

1. Who or what is God? . . . . . . . . . . . . .  3
2. Why did God create man & woman? . . . .  3
3. Why was I born? . . . . . . . . . . . . . . .  4
4. Why are there so many religions?  Which one is really "right?" . . . . . . . . . . .  4
5. Why does the world as we know it exist? .  5
6. What is mysticism? . . . . . . . . . . . . . .  5
7. Do we really have free will?  If there is an ultimate destiny that we are supposed to get closer to God, why do we have choices other than those that will bring us there? . . . . . . . . . . . . . . . . . .  6
8. What is prayer? Does it really work? . . . .  7
9. Do prayers come true? . . . . . . . . . . . .  8
10. How can I make my life into a prayer? . .  9

11. Why weren't we born more aware of our spiritual potential? .............. 9
12. For my spiritual progress, does this mean I should turn away from organized religion? ........................ 10
13. Often, we are taught those who do not believe the same as us are incorrect and unless they change shall be punished by God. Do we have a duty to try and correct their view? ................ 11
14. Are all spiritual paths the same? ..... 11
15. How do I know when I am following "the right" spiritual path? ........... 12
16. Many claim this is a special age for spirituality. Why is it special? ......... 13
17. I hear that many spiritual people are awaiting the return of a Great Teacher. Is there one Great Teacher we should all be looking for? ....................... 14
18. Who are "hidden teachers" and what is their role in spiritual development? ... 15
19. Who are the servants of God? What is their function? ................. 16
20. What is the role of the clergy or holy men /women? .................... 16
21. What about the saints and prophets? Are they real? .................... 18
22. In our culture, who assumes the role of holy one? In more traditional cultures this was a central figure that people recognized easily. ................ 19
23. How can you claim there is a Plan for humanity? Just look at the mess out there; surely somebody is not doing their job. . 21

24. Spiritually what is the significance of a family grouping? ... 22
25. What is spiritual experience? Is spiritual experience the same as God? ... 23
26. How do I know if I have had a spiritual experience? ... 26
27. How can we know God? What exactly does this mean? ... 27
28. I am in a place where I am questioning spirituality and its place in my life. What is the next step? Are there set stages I must go through to measure my progress? How do I know if I am taking steps forward in the path? ... 27
29. Is the whole point of spiritual learning to become a holy man and woman? ... 29
30. Is there a life plan for me? How can I relate to life stages in a spiritual sense? ... 29
31. What exactly does submitting to the Light mean? ... 30
32. How does one learn to hear his inner voice? Is this the same as instinct or "gut feeling?" I am usually right when I follow my gut! ... 32
33. How do I go about finding a teacher to guide me? ... 33
34. Is following the Path the same as just living everyday life? How are individual experiences similar? ... 34
35. It is said that man is a microcosm. What does this saying mean and what is its significance to the spiritual traveler? ... 36
36. What is the nature of the spiritual journey? What is its outcome? ... 38

37. Why must we die? .............. 39
38. I am frightened please tell me something to help ease my fear. Why must the physical body decay and die? ......... 41
39. What is the truth about heaven and hell? . 42
40. Do souls come back or reincarnate? .... 43
41. Is there anything more I should know about reincarnation? People often talk about what's possible "When I come back in my next life..." Is this something that is actually possible? A soul contemplating the next lessons to be learned when it returns to the earth? ............. 44
42. Two concepts that go along with the discussion of reincarnation are the Law of Karma and the Law of Grace. Can you tell me more about these? ........ 48
43. Why aren't we consciously aware of our karmic debt to others? .......... 51
44. How do we get to work out karma with other people across incarnations? .... 52
45. What is the point of religious teaching, if some organized religion has caused us to be so in doubt as to our true spiritual purpose? .................. 53
46. What purpose does organized religion as we know it serve? ............. 55
47. Why does God allow so much suffering and destruction in the world? Why are tyrants and psychopaths free to destroy? 57
48. So if all this is true, and I have a real destiny in terms of my soul, how does free will choice fit into things? ........ 58
49. Are some things bad and others good? . 59

50. What is the learning we are to accomplish? Is it one major lesson and then we have mastered the meaning of life or is there more to it? . . . . . . . . . . . . . . . . .  60
51. In today's world, many are turning to drugs, sex and self-indulgent behavior. Why are people so destructive? . . . . . . . .  61
52. Why do some people remain in the darkness or depression for extended periods and not try to reach toward the Light? .  62
53. What of the one that is harmed or killed in this process? What about them? . . .  63
54. What is the effect of people lying, cheating and stealing? . . . . . . . . . . . . . . . .  63
55. Why can't learning be less painful? Can't we learn in another way? . . . . . . . . .  64
56. What is a miracle? How do they occur? .  65
57. How will the shift to universal higher consciousness occur? . . . . . . . . . . . . .  67
58. How do I go about finding the "missing ingredient?" . . . . . . . . . . . . . . . .  69
59. Until I achieve this inner understanding, what should I do? . . . . . . . . . . . . .  70
60. All this sounds like 'do gooder' stuff. How do I know this is not just another religion looking for followers? How do I know this is the "real" right answer for me? . . . . . . . . . . . . . . . . . . . . .  70
61. Can two things, seemingly different, be true at the same time? . . . . . . . . . . .  71
62. Why do bad things happen? Particularly to people who try to live good lives? . .  73

63. Many times we are faced with decisions and do not know if an action will turn out positive or negative. Can you suggest a criteria or measuring stick that is useful? .................... 75
64. Are some things dark and evil? Is there a devil? ....................... 76
65. How do I balance the physical, mental and spiritual in my day-to-day living? .... 77
66. How do the mind, body and spirit work together? ..................... 79
67. What is consciousness? .......... 80
68. This sort of learning seems totally beyond me. Can you make this simpler? .... 81
69. In some traditions, people withdraw from the world to increase spiritual learning. Some join a monastery. Should I do this? 82
70. What advice can you give for spiritual parents looking to raise spiritually aware children? ....................... 83
71. How does a soul come to know its destiny? 84
72. Rare is the day when I am not fearful or anxious about something. When this happens, I grow tense; all of this is very uncomfortable. How is fear helpful and what spiritual purpose does it serve? .. 86
73. Why do things change and seemingly remain in motion? .............. 88
74. Why is it important to give to others? Some religions request a percent of your wage as regular donation. ............ 88
75. Why do people disagree and start wars over religious beliefs? How can both sides be right? .................... 89

76. If I am dissatisfied with my path, how do I find another? . . . . . . . . . . . . . . . . 91
77. Each of the great faiths has a holy book. What can you say about them? . . . . . 93
78. How is it possible for each of the great faiths to work? I am still having trouble with this. . . . . . . . . . . . . . . . . . . 95
79. Are you saying that prayers being answered are simply the operation of natural laws? If they are so natural, why don't we all just know them? . . . . . . . . . . . . . . . 96
80. Some people are fond of quoting God as a justification for advocating certain action or beliefs. They urge God says this or God says that. Can you comment upon this? . . . . . . . . . . . . . . . . . . . . . 97
81. I have heard different versions of what the afterlife will be like. How can all of these versions be true? Which account is factual? . . . . . . . . . . . . . . . . . . 98
82. Recently our science has proven that each atom, for the most part, is comprised of empty space. Consequently what we perceive as solid is not completely solid at all. So if I am sitting in a chair, am I really sitting in a chair, or the idea of a chair? 100
83. How will the spiritual teaching vary based upon people's needs? Will I find teaching that speaks to me directly? . . . . . . 102
84. How is each soul unique and how does each soul become aware of its place in the universe? . . . . . . . . . . . . . . . . . 102
85. What role does religion play in keeping people healthy and free from illness? . . 104

86. Can you elaborate on free will and how this relates to the concept of a life by design? .................... 106
87. Is a spiritually completed person, one who has achieved God Consciousness, a God? This is what some traditions claim. .... 109
88. No matter what you assert, how can this be the way the world is supposed to be; it's a real mess out there. How will the mystical view help our modern world? Is there a place for mysticism in times like these? .................... 111
89. What does the term enlightenment mean? Is this the goal of the mystical process? . 112
90. In my inner development, how do I know if I am advancing? What criteria can be used to measure progress? ........ 114
91. What is the outcome of a life? And how does this relate to Judgment Day? .... 115
92. What is the relationship between giving and healthy selfishness? .......... 116
93. The other day, some missionaries came to my door and were trying to convert me to their way of thinking. They were very insistent. Am I supposed to be open to this sort of thing or just ignore it? .... 117
94. Is there a faster way to do all this? Do I absolutely have to go through all these lifetimes to achieve the ultimate goal of spiritual studies? .............. 119
95. Do I really need a teacher? I like the idea of being my own guide. I'd like to find what interests me, study it and then move on. Can this work as an approach for me? 120

96. All right, I understand all of this; there is a preparation that is required. However, I am impatient and want to get on with it. I wish to begin study with my teacher. What am I to do? . . . . . . . . . . . . . 121
97. I have been accepted by a teacher and they have provided a course of study. It does not seem similar to what you are talking about at all! What do you say to that? . 122
98. Within a spiritual context, it is possible to have two goals operating, when this carries to a third, something is lost. What does this mean? . . . . . . . . . . . . . . . 124
99. Is there more than one name for God? Is it significant to use this name over another? 125

## II Stories, Verses & Observations    127

    100. The Theologian . . . . . . . . . . . . . . . 129
    101. Accepting God . . . . . . . . . . . . . . . 130
    102. The River . . . . . . . . . . . . . . . . . . . 130
    103. Giant Bazaar . . . . . . . . . . . . . . . . 132
    104. The World . . . . . . . . . . . . . . . . . . 132
    105. World as Canvas . . . . . . . . . . . . . . 134
    106. Freedom To Choose . . . . . . . . . . . 134
    107. Prayer . . . . . . . . . . . . . . . . . . . . . . 134
    108. Beyond Knowledge . . . . . . . . . . . 135
    109. Be Not Shy . . . . . . . . . . . . . . . . . . 135
    110. Bird Cage . . . . . . . . . . . . . . . . . . . 136
    111. Let Your Soul Soar . . . . . . . . . . . . 136
    112. Higher Law . . . . . . . . . . . . . . . . . 137
    113. Opposites . . . . . . . . . . . . . . . . . . . 138
    114. The Heart . . . . . . . . . . . . . . . . . . . 139
    115. The Criteria . . . . . . . . . . . . . . . . . 140

116. Super Highway to God / Light . . . . . . 140
117. Raising a Candle . . . . . . . . . . . . . . 141
118. Prayer for the New Age . . . . . . . . . 142
119. He Shall Walk . . . . . . . . . . . . . . . . 143
120. The Prophecy . . . . . . . . . . . . . . . . 143
121. Unseen Guardians . . . . . . . . . . . . 145
122. The Designers . . . . . . . . . . . . . . . 145
123. The Servants . . . . . . . . . . . . . . . . 146
124. Rare Jewels . . . . . . . . . . . . . . . . . 148
125. Higher Service . . . . . . . . . . . . . . 148
126. The Exemplar . . . . . . . . . . . . . . . 149
127. Raising Better People . . . . . . . . . . 150
128. Choosing How to Live . . . . . . . . . . 151
129. Empty House . . . . . . . . . . . . . . . 152
130. Parents . . . . . . . . . . . . . . . . . . . . 153
131. Spiritual Experience . . . . . . . . . . . 154
132. Searching for Truth . . . . . . . . . . . 154
133. Quiet Part of the Soul . . . . . . . . . . 155
134. Spiritual Sight . . . . . . . . . . . . . . . 156
135. The Tapestry . . . . . . . . . . . . . . . . 157
136. Spiritual Learning Outcomes . . . . . . . 158
137. Book of Life . . . . . . . . . . . . . . . . . 160
138. About Your Plan . . . . . . . . . . . . . 160
139. Surrender . . . . . . . . . . . . . . . . . . 161
140. Complicating Religion . . . . . . . . . . 162
141. A Guru . . . . . . . . . . . . . . . . . . . 162
142. Signs of a Master . . . . . . . . . . . . . 163
143. Preparing For a Teacher . . . . . . . . . 163
144. Foundation of the Way . . . . . . . . . 165
145. Path of the Spiritual Traveler . . . . . . 166
146. Awake & Manifest . . . . . . . . . . . . 166
147. Service . . . . . . . . . . . . . . . . . . . . 167
148. Going Home . . . . . . . . . . . . . . . . 168
149. Child of the Universe . . . . . . . . . . 169

| | | |
|---|---|---|
| 150. Be Yourself | . . . . . . . . . . . . . . . . . | 170 |
| 151. Learn About Yourself | . . . . . . . . . . | 170 |
| 152. Death's Call | . . . . . . . . . . . . . . . . | 171 |
| 153. The Change | . . . . . . . . . . . . . . . . | 172 |
| 154. Ray of Light | . . . . . . . . . . . . . . . | 173 |
| 155. Serving Truth | . . . . . . . . . . . . . . | 173 |
| 156. Love & Fear | . . . . . . . . . . . . . . . | 174 |
| 157. Rebirth | . . . . . . . . . . . . . . . . . . | 174 |
| 158. Morning Air | . . . . . . . . . . . . . . . | 174 |
| 159. Giving | . . . . . . . . . . . . . . . . . . | 175 |
| 160. One Religion | . . . . . . . . . . . . . . . | 175 |
| 161. Divine Friction | . . . . . . . . . . . . . | 177 |
| 162. Bending of Will | . . . . . . . . . . . . . | 178 |
| 163. Prayer of Surrender | . . . . . . . . . . . | 179 |
| 164. School & Learning | . . . . . . . . . . . | 179 |
| 165. World as Classroom | . . . . . . . . . . | 180 |
| 166. World Sickness | . . . . . . . . . . . . . | 180 |
| 167. Inner Conflict | . . . . . . . . . . . . . . | 181 |
| 168. Reaching the First Stair | . . . . . . . . | 182 |
| 169. Sunrise & Set | . . . . . . . . . . . . . . | 182 |
| 170. The Heart Answers | . . . . . . . . . . . | 182 |
| 171. Evening Fire | . . . . . . . . . . . . . . . | 183 |
| 172. Faith & Knowing | . . . . . . . . . . . . | 183 |
| 173. Knowing | . . . . . . . . . . . . . . . . . | 184 |
| 174. Physical Form | . . . . . . . . . . . . . . | 185 |
| 175. Origins of Wisdom | . . . . . . . . . . . | 185 |
| 176. Talking to God / Light | . . . . . . . . . | 186 |
| 177. Greater Freedom | . . . . . . . . . . . . | 187 |
| 178. Hand of Fate | . . . . . . . . . . . . . . | 187 |
| 179. Inner Walls | . . . . . . . . . . . . . . . | 188 |
| 180. Process of Change | . . . . . . . . . . . | 189 |
| 181. Always Getting What You Want | . . . . . | 189 |
| 182. What If | . . . . . . . . . . . . . . . . . . | 190 |
| 183. To Be | . . . . . . . . . . . . . . . . . . . | 191 |

| | |
|---|---|
| 184. The Books | 192 |
| 185. Bottled Water | 193 |
| 186. Higher Reality | 194 |
| 187. Time Dragging On | 194 |
| 188. Be a Beetle | 194 |
| 189. When You Are Flying | 195 |
| 190. Enlightenment | 196 |
| 191. Judgment Day Song | 196 |
| 192. Higher Forms | 197 |
| 193. What is Sufism? | 198 |
| 194. The Teaching | 200 |
| 195. The Prince | 201 |
| **Epilogue: A Call to Hearts** | **207** |
| **Books By Stewart Bitkoff** | **209** |

# Part I

# Questions & Answers

# 1. Who or what is God?

God is the Light of the universe and is the mother and father of us all. God is present in everything and is the underlying unity of all things. God is the life force and binds together the worlds. God is all loving and merciful, and a piece of God, a spark of energy called the Heart, is in everyone.

God is greater than all creation and exists beyond the universe. While we may know and experience God, many aspects of God are beyond our experience and remain a mystery.

In our age, science has defined God as a supra-energy force that is part of everything and connects all things. Mystics have perceived this reality and used it for countless centuries: bringing Light to the spiritual darkness.

For some, the word / name "God" has many negative connotations; if this is true for you, substitute the word, "Light." This may help you travel through these pages; remember it is the Light which dissipates spiritual darkness.

# 2. Why did God create man & woman?

Man and woman were created as God's representatives on earth. A human being is the meeting of the spiritual, mental, psychic (emotional) and physical realms. Man is destined to reign in kingship, believe it or not, in this realm along with God as a co-creator of reality. The traveler who has mastered himself and reigns supreme in his own kingdom, is master of all worlds.

Man and woman are reflections of all the different expressions of God.

## 3. Why was I born?

We take on the physical form so we might better know God, create our own reality, and serve God. Here in the earth phase, we can learn, create and experience many beautiful and wonderful things and accelerate our spiritual journey back to God. The contrast between the earthly and spiritual provides a friction that pushes us to question our existence and the meaning of life. This friction increases our learning and understanding.

## 4. Why are there so many religions? Which one is really "right?"

God is One.

However, the many religions exist because people and cultures are different; these differences in religious form exist to help people better understand who they are and where they came from.

In this matter there is both an internal and external reality. The internal reality is the spiritual experience of God and, for all religious forms; the closer you get to God, the more this experience is the same. Externally religious forms differ; religion puts on "different clothes," so to speak, because the social climate and people's needs vary.

Imagine religion as a beautiful woman. One day she travels to a land where it is cold. By necessity she puts on a fur garment to keep warm. The next week, as circumstances dictate, she travels to another land where it is much hotter. In order to adjust, she sheds the fur and adorns a cotton dress.

Depending upon the day you met her; you would describe her outward appearance differently. Yet beneath the clothing, she is the same, beautiful woman and any difference in appearance is superficial.

It is like this with religion. People get caught up with the externals, argue about the clothing and forget about the core truths.

# 5. Why does the world as we know it exist?

The world is a magnificent cornucopia, filled with wondrous and delightful items. Here we can find exactly what we are looking for. If we seek enjoyment of the senses, there are many opportunities. Similarly if we seek to learn and draw closer to our higher self, this opportunity exists as well.

In part, the earth phase of our existence is an opportunity to learn, create and experience all the parts of self and grow closer to that which we wish to become.

# 6. What is mysticism?

Mysticism is the process by which one studies or learns about the mysteries or mystery traditions. Within each of the great faiths, there is an inner, hidden teaching that is transcendent and unifying. The reason this teaching is hidden is that in order to study it, a number of factors have to be in place. Until recently, these factors were not publicly stated or no attempts have been made to make them publicly understood.

When viewed from a distance, these criteria are applicable to any human endeavor. Suppose we want to learn about fly-fishing. We would have to find out what time the class is starting, where it is being held, who is teaching the class and what preparations / materials are necessary. Is the class for beginners or more advanced students?

It is the same with mystical studies, however, one other additional factor is operating. This is termed "sincerity" and relates to the intention of the student. If the student wishes to align with Truth, not for individual gain, but for its own sake; these are the students who attain knowledge, and it is this sincerity the teacher is drawn to and recognizes in the student. Because of this inner condition, traditionally the teacher finds the student. Together they unlock the mysteries of the spiritual path.

## 7. Do we really have free will? If there is an ultimate destiny that we are supposed to get closer to God, why do we have choices other than those that will bring us there?

Each person has the ability to choose and create. This is what sets us apart from other creatures. We can choose and create our own reality every moment of the day; and influence our life and world as co-creator.

Within ourselves we have a magic wand and can turn each day into a beautiful or frightening experience. Our imagination and ability to make thoughts come true is the magical element. Through our consciousness, we can create all sorts of things and must be careful to make useful and wise decisions.

Choices that are in front of us are just that – choices. On a Higher Level, there is really no such thing as a good or bad choice; only choices that bring us closer to God or further away from God.

On a day to day level, people can and do make bad choices all the time. Or make choices because it may serve a personal need. Such as doing what your boss wants you to do which may not serve the greater good but preserves your job and income for your family.

Deep down inside, we know what will result from the choices we make. The skill lies in being able to tap that knowledge that already exists and use it for a Higher Purpose.

# 8. What is prayer? Does it really work?

Prayer is a song that arises from our heart and tells the sweet tale of love. Not love as we have ever experienced it, but a deep, transcendent love that spans the ages. It is a whisper that comes from the depth of our soul and a melody through which we can share secrets, weaknesses, dreams and desires with God.

In prayer there must be no compulsion; it is not

something that can be forced or taught. Real prayer is as natural as breathing; it is a song, an expression of our eternal self. Most of us learn through our religious upbringing that prayer is done by rote. We memorize our prayers and say them every night before bed. Then we can ask God to give us something we really want, and he will listen. Yet, this is not the higher prayer; the higher prayer is helping and praying for others, as God's servant.

If you can learn to make your life a prayer, every moment you can sing the song of creation. Yes, prayer used in this form can assist us in co-creation of our reality with God. It works.

## 9. Do prayers come true?

Yes, but not all prayers and not always in the time frame desired. How are prayers evaluated into those that will be answered and those that will not?

Attached to prayer is consciousness and energy. Under certain circumstances, this energy interacts with the potential inherent in a situation, generating an action. To work, prayer energy must be offered up with purity of intention and love; when that intention is aligned with Truth and the potential of the situation, prayers do come true. When they are not, they don't.

Of recent interest is the research occurring around the phenomena of distant healing. In double blind studies, healers pray and send healing energy to the person that is ill. Some of these studies have generated remarkable healing results. Yes, in our time, we have scientifically validated 'old time' religious practice and we are gaining data about the universe and physical laws we do not completely understand.

# 10. How can I make my life into a prayer?

Making your life into a prayer means living life for God and making our actions an extension of the Divine Will. This is part of the heritage of humanity. What we need, and most of us are missing, is the guidance of a qualified teacher.

While real prayer cannot be taught, and is an expression of our inner self, what we can learn from a teacher is how to refine our spiritual capacities so the inner song might come forward.

This teaching or spiritual preparation requires the interaction between a student who is correctly aligned, a teacher who has completed the journey, and finally the blessings, what is known as "Baraka," inherent in a spiritual path.

# 11. Why weren't we born more aware of our spiritual potential?

Actually we are born totally aware of our spiritual potential. However we are quickly taught to disregard this essential aspect to our nature. We are taught about the restrictions of the rational mind, at the expense of our spiritual core.

By design it is trained out of us at an early age so we can get on with more practical things. Then, for the majority of us the spiritual experience or religion we are given is little more than a social indoctrination system based upon reward and punishment. Also, people are taught to rely upon the religious system and its representatives, instead of developing their own inner potential. This reliance can become a subtle form of control.

In this age people are again turning inward to awaken that which has been hidden from them. We are returning to knowledge that we were born with.

## 12. For my spiritual progress, does this mean I should turn away from organized religion?

No! In fact, for many the great religions are the bridge that leads to the Divine.

If you are Muslim, seek to be a better Muslim. Similarly if you are a Jew or Catholic seek to be a better Jew or Catholic.

Each of the great religions, as their spiritual teachings are followed, provides a path to God.

Over time, the traveler must learn to follow the inner teaching or heart of their religion, and as needed, discard the "useless clothing."

## 13. Often, we are taught those who do not believe the same as us are incorrect and unless they change shall be punished by God. Do we have a duty to try and correct their view?

First of all, God is not a punishing force in the lives of humans. We must learn to let go of this conditioning. Think of God as a father. Does a father love only some of his children? Of course not! Then, the next question to ask is, are we not all children of God?

Before there was organized religion, how did people worship? Were these millions all in error and abandoned by their Father / Mother? The answer, of course, is no.

To every place and time is a path or religion that fits a person's needs. Look to a person's heart and their actions; a good, loving person, who makes the world a better place, is a servant of God and has a religion to follow. Let God evaluate the measure of their lives; God's mercy is without limit.

## 14. Are all spiritual paths the same?

No two things in the universe are the same. Even identical twins have differences. While all spiritual paths have the capacity to educate and help the traveler advance, some emphasize inner development, while others emphasize social responsibility and ceremonial ritual. While these externals are important, because they meet our individual needs, they are not inner knowing or perception of reality.

The thing to remember about all of the various paths to enlightenment is that they all end up in the same place.

## 15. How do I know when I am following "the right" spiritual path?

You know this by listening to your heart while you are not afraid, threatened or coerced by others. In time as spiritual capacities develop, you will receive proof of a different sort.

All authentic spiritual paths teach about learning, service and responsibility to self and others. Authentic paths celebrate life and the importance of not causing harm.

Ask yourself if your path brings you closer to the Light, life force or God. Or does your path distance you from your higher self and serving humanity? You will know by how you feel about the answers to these questions.

On your path, if others want money, allegiance or specific behaviors (out of fear and reward), then it is best for you to separate from them for a time. Use this time to decide if this is the path for you. If others resist this period of self-examination, be wary.

## 16. Many claim this is a special age for spirituality. Why is it special?

We live in an age when technologically, as a global community, we have the power to create a wondrous world or destroy ourselves. Are third world countries' struggles and hunger to be ignored so that only the industrialized society can materially benefit? Or do we come together and share our collective wealth and potential? That is the challenge that faces humanity at this critical time. Do the interests of some override the interests of many? What criteria or moral yardstick do we have to make decisions about these problems?

This is indeed a special age. As a global community we have the capacity, for the most part, to eliminate hunger and disease. Also we are examining spiritual experience, free of social censure, with scientific interest and wonder. Yet where do we go from here? Do we have more of the same? Or does something more advanced emerge on a global level?

Today many are turning toward non-traditional spiritual systems for individual answers and are seeking more than the prevailing self-interest and greed that seems to drive so many people. That thirst for "something more" is driving many of us to not only question the status quo, but also to find some answers.

After a period of preparation, authentic spiritual teaching provides the traveler with an internal yardstick that helps balance the needs of the individual and many. This internal indicator is a spiritual capacity to know what is right. In part that is the goal of spiritual preparation. Authentic paths create individuals who are better able to serve themselves and others. Internally all travelers have the capacity to balance the spiritual and physical.

As we seek to improve ourselves and serve others, we realize that the world is truly made better one person at a time.

## 17. I hear that many spiritual people are awaiting the return of a Great Teacher. Is there one Great Teacher we should all be looking for?

It is prophecy that the Great Teacher will return and again turn hearts upward in remembrance. As circumstance dictates, the Great Teacher will make public the Teaching. It is the same spiritual teaching that is updated into a modern form so that people in today's society can understand. The teaching is that all the great religions are one and spring from the same source. Mankind has this knowledge but has simply forgotten, hence the need for a Great Teacher to communicate this message. We are all brothers and sisters and are most distant from our lasting spiritual nature when we forget to experience the reality of God's love and mercy.

When we experience the Light on a daily basis, it makes us whole and better able to serve others.

Until the Great Teacher emerges, however, turn inward toward God, and ask to drink of God's Love and Mercy. For in the spiritual realm, there is no time and distance and the teaching can be made manifest at any time or place.

# 18. Who are "hidden teachers" and what is their role in spiritual development?

The world is never without hidden teachers. They are in each country, town and city. Like a corporation there is a hierarchy with different responsibilities for these teachers. Tradition has it that at any given time the number of teachers is fixed and they are in spiritual contact with each other.

In part their job is to reflect the Light into the world and guard the Plan for humanity. Without their efforts the world would cease to exist; the Light is a life giving force and is the essential nutrient of humanity.

The Plan for humanity is to evolve to a higher spiritual condition and, in this realm, join God in the creative process. The Plan is accomplished one person at a time and the guardians of this Plan are the hidden teachers.

When there is a design emerging that deviates or threatens the Plan, these teachers and others take action. The Plan will unfold over millennia.

In every city and town there are those who are the instruments of the unseen world. Their purpose is to be the hands of God / Light on this planet. They move with the Higher Law and actively guide the destiny of humanity. These are God's Servants. You find them everywhere, operating quietly amongst us. When there is someone in your life who leads by example in a quiet way, and helps you to see life from a spiritual perspective, this is likely a hidden teacher. It is quite possible that you have met or know one already.

## 19. Who are the servants of God? What is their function?

The servants of God are those individuals who have completed the spiritual journey and through grace are able to serve the Divine Will. Each servant performs different functions.

As indicated earlier, these servants are organized into a hierarchy. At the moment, the spiritual traveler remembers and says the prayer (of submission) with sincerity, they have joined 'the organization.'

Like an efficient corporation there are departments or sections. Some of these functions include reflecting the Light into the physical world; assuring the Plan for humanity; and teaching. However, the servants of God also have roles in day to day life as we know it. This spiritual structure has existed since the beginning of time and the great religious teachers, according to tradition, are part of this organization and effort.

Like the tip of an iceberg, only a small portion of this work is visible. Without these servants, the physical world, as we know it, would not exist.

## 20. What is the role of the clergy or holy men / women?

Originally spiritual teachings did not require intermediaries to intercede to the Deity on another's behalf. As teachings developed into formal religions, the role of priest developed to help educate, and assist people to communicate with their God. In the historical development of spreading a spiritual teaching, the role of clergy was used to help spread the initial revelation. Later, the role of clergy expanded adding sociological, service, and educational components.

It is important for each of us to decide if going to a priest, sheik, or rabbi, to intercede on our behalf with God or Truth is helpful. Among their number, there are many dedicated and sincere people who wish to be of service. For those who do not find intercession by clergy helpful, they might find assistance from another member of their community. Most religions or spiritual traditions, acknowledge the presence of holy men or holy women. These are people who have developed knowledge and awareness of the Divine. Along with this knowledge comes a degree of spiritual ability which is needed to execute their function. These people may or may not be part of the organized clergy and are able, through inner perception, to communicate with Truth. This may be the kind of person who is more helpful to you.

In our society, there is a visible absence of the role of spiritual teacher. Because of this void many have turned away from religion and are looking for another vehicle to enrich spiritual learning. Hence the reawakening of interest in spiritual experience, self-discovery and, by extension, the ancient mystery traditions that we are discussing here.

Keep in mind, just because you do not see a thing, it does not mean it no longer exists. In the evening, the sun is still shining. In the spiritual realm, because of the nature of their work, these people are not visible as spiritual teachers but as regular, everyday people.

## 21. What about the saints and prophets? Are they real?

In every endeavor there are people who are gifted and perceive what others do not. They have extraordinary capacity and much to offer. For example, most people enjoy music and can even perform or create simple pieces. Yet rare is the person who through training and opportunity has the capacity to become a Mozart. Someone like this is born with genius and over time this expands, matures and is shared with the world.

It is the same in spiritual studies. While each can learn and raise their spirituality, some are born with greater capacity that engenders a wider role. These great souls enter the earth phase to share their knowledge with others and raise the consciousness of society.

Within each spiritual tradition, there are the great teachers or servants of God. These are the prophets, saints and people of wisdom. Traditionally the inceptor of a great faith is termed a prophet. In part, the prophet's role is to initiate a pathway to God or Truth. Prophets are vested with grace or "Baraka," from God, to do this and have a wider mission.

Traditionally a saint follows in the footsteps of a prophet and the saint's mission is less broad. Typically a saint renews or emphasizes a specific aspect of a tradition. The saint also receives grace from God and has a defined spiritual mission, though on a lesser scale than a prophet.

People of wisdom, as they are called, are those who are in tune with Truth, and come to help raise consciousness. Their mission is more confined than either a prophet or saint; each town, village and city has people of wisdom. They help reflect the Light and attune humanity to Truth.

Spiritual capacity, talent and mission are dependent upon many factors. Each of the servants of God has a specific role and in order to accomplish it develop certain capacities. To perform their function, each operates through the grace inherent in their path.

## 22. In our culture, who assumes the role of holy one? In more traditional cultures this was a central figure that people recognized easily.

In traditional cultures an important figure was the holy man or holy woman. Often they advised the chief, understood and prescribed medicine, and helped pass along the oral history of the tribe and had an inner connection with universal wisdom and Truth. When a difficult situation arose, this individual was key in helping decide the direction or outcome. Daily they were consulted on a variety of issues.

Today the diverse role and function of the holy one has been spread among a team of specialists. For guidance, we go to a priest, counselor, doctor, psychologist, historian, politician or lawyer. Because of the complexity of some issues, the specialist may not even live in our community, and to consult with them we make an appointment, months in advance, travel to get the advice / treatment and pay a fee.

This model has plus and minuses. Specialists because of training have information and expertise not available to others. In some ways, these people are essential and our culture cannot be without them. However by separating out problems and going to others for solutions, we lose sight of the fact that, for the most part, it is possible to manage daily concerns ourselves. With the "holy one" model, a majority of issues can be solved by one person, who is readily accessible, knows us and is part of our tribe / family.

In both models, there is an over reliance upon others. While it is important in today's technical world to have the option to work / consult with a specialist, generally, we have forgotten our own individual potential represented by the wise one. With training, we can become our own source of wisdom and through enhanced inner perception manage our own daily issues, consulting with specialists as indicated.

Gradually we are returning to a model of self-reliance and individual responsibility. We are shifting away from dependence upon others and searching for inner wisdom to manage our lives. Tomorrow each person will be their own wise one, consulting with specialists far less frequently and only when required. This is the next stage in the evolutionary process.

## 23. How can you claim there is a Plan for humanity? Just look at the mess out there; surely somebody is not doing their job.

Many would assert the world is in chaos and daily we continue to destroy ourselves. Further the idea of a spiritual plan for humanity is absurd; just look at our track record and the growing materialism, addictions, and physical and sexual abuse / exploitation of our young. Additionally, historically, so-called spiritual leaders have been responsible through war and greed for some of our greatest suffering. In fact today many religious organizations continue as some of the richest corporations on earth.

This description of humanity's self-destructive capacity is true; however it describes only part of the picture. It neglects our higher nature and the unselfish efforts of billions. For example none of us would be here without the love and care of parents, friends and relatives. The fact that religious leaders start wars for their own interest does not take away the fact that many continue, in their role of clergy, to serve the higher law, fight for reform and help whenever they can.

From a spiritual perspective, events and experiences are neither bad nor good. Events must be evaluated using the criteria of learning, service and how each brought us closer to our higher self.

Spiritually, suffering is a type of friction with the potential to speed our learning. On another level it may be an inevitable outcome of the situation causing harm. What we choose to do about suffering, on an individual and global level, is part of our learning on the spiritual path.

# 24. Spiritually what is the significance of a family grouping?

Each of us is a member of two families: the birth / marriage family and the larger, human family. In both, meaningful membership and participation is essential to balanced development. Each person must feel they are loved and protected, and have the opportunity to express, without fear, who they are. Each is a unique soul and has something to contribute and learn.

In a family there is a connection which occurs on many levels: it may be biological, emotional, spiritual, or a combination of these.

Spiritually the members of a birth / marriage family have entered the earth phase together to learn from each other. On an inner level, their souls are connected. Sometimes the lessons are painful and other times joyous. This connection extends beyond time and space.

Similarly humanity is one family. We have all come from the same source (God) and one day will return home after experiencing many worlds. Spiritually each person is connected and humanity, gradually, will awaken to this elemental truth. When this occurs, the world will be much different.

Families and communities are encouraged to worship together. This communal practice is advocated for more than social and emotional reasons. Spiritually when souls focus together, the spiritual energy that is produced is life giving, integrating and transcendent.

Often, this communal energy is different than what can be experienced as an individual. In those moments, it is possible to spiritually know and experience the reason for existence. When the soul, is at peace with the Source there are no questions, only answers. Those moments are transcendent and become the basis and direction of the next steps in a person's life.

On the spiritual path, there is another family. This is the family of believers. Souls come together to support each other in the work and make spiritual progress that can only be accomplished in groups. This experience of group energy and accomplishment is similar in other endeavors. Sometimes those who work together in a vocational setting become so close they characterize their experience as a special and familial one. Sports team members who work together and accomplish success, describe this same special energy and bonding.

# 25. What is spiritual experience? Is spiritual experience the same as God?

Each person is a world of many levels. In this age we are just beginning to experience and explore the complexity of consciousness and spiritual experience. Historically other cultures have also studied what we now call consciousness and spiritual experience. Some of these cultures have hundreds of words to describe the complexity of this experience. Today, we have a few terms of our own (i.e., states and stations).

One obvious limitation is that it is impossible to describe in written or verbal words the intricacies of a multi-level experience. We may get close to the sensation but it is not the same as actually experiencing it. A spiritual experience occurs on many levels simultaneously in our body and consciousness.

As an example, poets and songsters have been trying for eons to describe the complexity of romantic love. At best their words and songs are an approximation of the experience of being in love. Further, over time, this experience changes, grows and becomes deeper. While words can get you close they are not the same. Once you have tasted of authentic spiritual experience, you realize words may take you to the door, but cannot get you inside the room.

To further confuse matters, different religions use different words to describe what is believed to be the same or similar experience (i.e., peace of God, Unity and Nirvana). These peak experiences must be viewed within the context of a specific system. It is also true that the closer the traveler gets to the Source, regardless of the path, the more similar becomes the unifying experience.

Spiritual experiences are distinguished from emotional or physical experiences by the level of spiritual energy involved. These experiences are not similar to other experiences and involve a different part of our consciousness. Also these experiences happen so you can learn something and move forward along the path.

In the beginning of a mystic's training, there is a period where the student is provided with a unique experience that opens the door and awakens the soul. This experience is akin to feeling one with all living things. In part it is a foretaste of things to come, displays the direction to travel, and helps place the student firmly on the path.

Some think this is the end product and are content, because it is a sublime experience, to try and repeat this over and over. Yet it is only a beginning and there are numerous other experiences along the way.

Spiritual experience is not the same as God. It is the experience of the essence from which we all came, through a part of this essence that is the center (heart) of our soul. Remember that which enters the physical universe is different than that which exists outside the universe. God is greater than all of creation.

The following is an old example to explain this. While it is possible to know a great deal about a potter by examining a bowl, we cannot know the potter entirely. We may hold the bowl and feel its texture, examine it under different lights, and over time feel artistically one with it and the potter. However no matter how many aspects of the potter we experience through his creation, the potter is greater and more complex than this one work. In time, the potter can go on to create all sorts of things which may be totally different. Each of these creations has aspects of the potter in them, but under examination do not explain all that is required to make the piece. For example, where did the idea of design and choice of color come from? How did the artist learn his craft? Over time what were the factors that influenced him? You cannot get all of this from one bowl or studying the artist's life. Always the potter remains different and greater, more complex, than the bowl he creates.

# 26. How do I know if I have had a spiritual experience?

Our essential nature is that of spirit and on one level all experience is spiritual experience. Emotions, thoughts and consciousness flow from the spirit into the body. Spirit needs the physical to unfold and we are many levels of consciousness.

Along the spiritual path to self-discovery there are thousands of states of consciousness; which are markedly different from everyday awareness and our thoughts / desires about participating in the world. This consciousness is akin to cable TV as opposed to regular TV, where the reception and programming is stronger, clearer and brighter.

A common beginning spiritual experience is the experience of oneness and recognizing your connection to all living things. In this state, everyday consciousness is temporarily overwhelmed by the spiritual essence and you merge with the Essential in all things. Here you celebrate your primal self and its kinship with everything else. This experience is an experience of the underlying unity in the universe and your own connection to the life force. An aspect of this life force and energy is within you, and sings to its own spirituality.

You will know you are having a spiritual experience because it will be different than any experience you have had before. By opening yourself to this new experience you permit a direct, personal and enhanced way of understanding to enter into your consciousness. It may have the capacity to change you in a subtle but essential way.

## 27. How can we know God? What exactly does this mean?

It is possible to know a little about God through the Light. Through training and grace, we are able to have a glimpse of that aspect of the Divine that is present in the created universe.

While we may gather a fleeting glimpse, it is not the same as the actual sensation of being unified with God. This is what we speak of when we talk about knowing God.

## 28. I am in a place where I am questioning spirituality and its place in my life. What is the next step? Are there set stages I must go through to measure my progress? How do I know if I am taking steps forward in the path?

As with any endeavor there are levels of ability that are dependent upon a variety of factors. These include individual capacity, training, experience and good luck or fortune.

As an example, let us discuss learning how to swim. In order for learning to occur several things must be in place. You need someone who wants to learn, a teacher who is able to teach and a place (i.e., pool, lake) where swimming can occur. Also there must be an interaction between the student, the teacher and subject being taught. The student must want to learn, the teacher must have skills and correct temperament to impart the lesson and the setting must be conducive to learning. Over time, as the student progresses, he has certain experiences, completes various swimming exercises, and moves along the learning continuum.

It is similar along the path of spiritual learning and progress is dependent upon an interaction between the student, the teacher and the grace inherent in the path. Students have the capacity to learn at different rates and understand at different levels what the teacher is trying to impart.

The teacher is one who has traveled the path to completion and has been selected to help others make the journey. Not all travelers who have completed the journey are designated as teachers.

The magical element in all of this is the grace, or Baraka, inherent in the path. Without this, none would successfully make the journey. It is this magical element the teacher uses to call the student and begin the journey. The spiritual Baraka of the path ensures that it remains a viable road to completion.

The different stages of the journey refer, in part, to the activation of specific capacities and spiritual centers within the student. In order for these spiritual centers to be activated without harm to the student, this activation must occur under the guidance of a teacher. To activate these centers prematurely, through spiritual exercises that are not correctly prescribed, can result in lasting harm to the student.

As with swimming, in spiritual studies, there are beginners, intermediate and advanced practitioners of all kinds.

## 29. Is the whole point of spiritual learning to become a holy man and woman?

The point of spiritual growth is to produce the completed human being: a person, who is in tune with the Source, participates in the everyday world, and consciously serves the Divine Will.

Each person is created with a wide range of talents and interests; the point of life is to express these abilities in the world and do this as a servant of the Light. We were not created to go off someplace, live the life of a recluse and contemplate our navel!

The world needs better people who are in tune with the many aspects of themselves and work to make the world a better place. Some do this as corporate workers, others as parents, and some as disabled people in the local social service program. Each has something to offer the world and the world benefits when each submits to the Light.

## 30. Is there a life plan for me? How can I relate to life stages in a spiritual sense?

In some traditions it is believed that each soul before entering into the physical realm, prepares a life plan. In this plan are delineated the learning and experiences which are necessary to assist the soul in completing its life's work or mission. To assist the soul in preparing its life plan, other spiritual entities in the form of teachers provide guidance and direction. To ensure success, these and other souls are available to help throughout the soul's incarnation in this realm.

As the soul's life plan unfolds, the soul goes through various stages, learning and aspects of the mission are completed. In this belief system, a soul incarnates for a specific reason or mission, it is also recognized that the learning is multi-level and effect of one's life upon others, potentially, is unlimited. Each stage in the soul's journey is filled with variety and opportunity to learn, serve and recognize the One Reality.

However, in practical terms, within each season there are opportunities to embrace the various dimensions to our existence. For example, in adulthood there is a period when we prepare for career, enter into a career, and depending upon circumstance, alter aspects of this career. This life is filled with energy, motion, creativity and change.

# 31. What exactly does submitting to the Light mean?

The Light is that aspect of the Source, or Divine, that presents itself in the created universe. It is the life giving force, or in some traditions "Logos," that is the underlying unity in the universe. The Light is most easily understood as that which illuminates.

Imagine that which is greater than the universe extending a part of itself into the universe. By necessity, that which is greater than created forms would have to undergo some transformation to take on a physical form. This entity is termed the Light and is perceived by our spiritual center.

Daily each of us makes many decisions. Usually these decisions occur on a conscious level and involve what we have come to know as the elements of logical, quantitative and imaginative thought. However our consciousness is more than what we can think about, feel or imagine. We are also of spirit. When one submits to the Light, this element of spiritual consciousness is gradually added.

We can begin to understand a little about what submitting to the Light means by reflecting on experiences with our "gut feelings." Often, when faced with a decision, how often are we right when we just "had a feeling?" Sometimes we ignore all of the logical and quantitative thoughts that cross our minds. We can't quite tell why, except that we just had a feeling. And sometimes, we follow it – often it is the right thing to do. Although not quite the same as following the Light, we can begin to imagine the surrender necessary in order to do so.

Our inner consciousness, or spiritual awareness, operates in conjunction with other capacities. When our emotions, rational thought and spiritual perception are aligned; then, we make decisions that are based upon the higher need and destiny of the universe.

## 32. How does one learn to hear his inner voice? Is this the same as instinct or "gut feeling?" I am usually right when I follow my gut!

In order for this to occur, it is not a matter of adding something but removing what stands in the way.

In most, every day consciousness is filled with repeating thoughts, desires and patterns. These are the thoughts our culture has taught us are important and necessary for daily living. Many of these thoughts focus upon survival, self-interest and maintaining the status quo. Usually, these thoughts lead to actions that are essential to personal and community survival.

Beneath these layers of thoughts and feelings, which are necessary to participate in the physical world, there is another mode of awareness. In order to perceive spiritually, the noise of daily life must be quieted: over time and with guidance we learn to hear this inner whisper. This whisper can be heard when the other desires and thoughts are stilled for a time. The ability to still every day thoughts and desires is within us, it is part of us, but for most it must be activated through the intervention of a teacher.

This capacity to hear the inner voice comes and goes based upon the needs of the situation. Our everyday thoughts and desires are necessary for our life in the world. The spiritual consciousness exists to integrate and make whole the interplay of factors in our lives. By turning inward, and stilling the noises of daily life, we hear the inner voice and this helps us with decisions and life problems.

Remember we were created to live and participate in the world. Spiritual awareness is a capacity that we can integrate to help with the problems of daily life. We can gain a more complete, holistic view and the ability to see events from a higher perspective. This is part of the birthright of humanity and, for most, is awakened by one of the teachers we meet when we embark upon the spiritual path.

This can only happen when there is a correct alignment of the student, the teacher and the path. The student must be prepared and relatively free of self-interest; the student must be able to listen objectively to what the teacher offers. For most, this is impossible; most students believe they already know and have everything they need.

Also, we cannot will ourselves to be free from self-interest. It is a natural development that occurs when we engage in true service and when we devote ourselves to the pursuit of inner knowledge.

## 33. How do I go about finding a teacher to guide me?

Traditionally while the student may be in search of a teacher and present himself for teaching, the teacher must decide if the student is ready. The teacher is able to evaluate the student's inner capacity. Not all would-be students, spiritually, are ready to learn; they may believe they are ready and want this badly, but the correct factors must be present.

The would-be student must be able to put aside, for a time, notions of what he or she believes is the teaching and be able to experience what is actually being taught. Also the student must be free of self-interest and seek the teaching for its own sake. Internally the student should not desire what the teaching will bring in the way of rewards and capacities. Through love and service, the student must wish to be one with the teaching.

It is only the teacher, through inner capacity, who can discern the student's sincerity in this matter. Often the student is unaware of his or her own motives. Through training and experience, the student learns to perceive his / her own limitations.

The teacher through directing the Light awakens the student's own inner capacity. This capacity has been dormant and the teacher calls this capacity to awaken. By being in the teacher's presence, and through the direction of the Light, the student experiences his or her own inner capacity. Slowly the teacher shows the student the goal; over time and further training, the student learns to travel by him or herself.

## 34. Is following the Path the same as just living everyday life? How are individual experiences similar?

From a spiritual perspective, the point of life is to make the world better, while growing closer to the Source. So that the traveler does not stray too far from this goal, the path was created. The path is the interaction between the traveler, the guide and Baraka or spiritual grace which gives the path its vibrancy; each is essential and combines, under the correct circumstances, to provide a vehicle which results in the completed person.

On the path, each person's experience is both unique and collective. Each person is an individual expression of the Divine element. Also, as a member of humanity, each person is similar to others and aspects to the learning are similar.

Experiences and exercises are prescribed and given. Some are unique to the individual and others are communal. For example, the individual prays, or meditates, as an individual and as a member of a spiritual community; during the course of instruction, these experiences are both singular and collective.

Along the path, the part that ensures the student does not get lost, is the guidance of the teacher and grace under which he / she operates. Spiritually the teacher is able to monitor the student's progress and knows whatever is necessary to assist the student. This knowledge or spiritual capacity comes about as a result of the spiritual grace of the path. It is a capacity that exists, in part, outside the teacher and moves through him / her as necessary to guide the traveler.

Each of the great religions is a path to completion. Present in all these forms are the elements defined above. Each great path has a historical period when most active. Over time, as paths become physically more distant from the point of their inception, they age; repetition and systematization set in and they become less vibrant. Then, as God Wills, a teacher appears to restore and give life to that which has fallen into disarray.

The mystical path is always dependent upon a living teacher. The teacher prescribes individually for the student and if repetition and systematization are used, it is for a specific purpose and limited time. It is the teacher's function to know what each student needs.

While all of this is happening, we are living our everyday lives. We are going to work, raising a family, eating – all of the things that comprise our day-to-day. The spiritual path is parallel to what we have come to know as our everyday reality. But as we learn and grow on our spiritual path, our everyday reality will change!

## 35. It is said that man is a microcosm. What does this saying mean and what is its significance to the spiritual traveler?

In relation to the larger cosmos and God, man / woman is the smaller universe. It is believed that when a traveler has mastered his own kingdom / universe (self), he is master of the larger.

Science has proven what the ancients have known for millennia. Man is a small universe, with billions of factors working together. Man is made up of billions of cells and trillions of atoms; he is the by-product of millions of years of evolution and is a highly complex and sometimes contradictory being.

Mystically man is consciousness and the coming together of three realms. The physical, mental (or psychic) and spiritual realms all exist simultaneously within man's consciousness. The terms spirit and soul, in common use, are interchangeable and sometimes confusing. In our discussion, what is important is that we recognize and develop our latent spiritual capacity.

Additionally it is believed that while man simultaneously exists on three planes, and the higher soul is always one with the Source or higher impulse, usually this aspect of consciousness is blocked by lower stimuli (physical, mental and emotional) and the inner journey consists of learning to push aside lower impulses so the higher might be heard. We are always in tune with the Source, but because of inner distractions have forgotten how to listen to the inner whisper.

The three realms coincide with our modern discussion about physical, mental (thought and emotional) and spiritual awareness. Generally man is believed to have all three levels of consciousness and energy present and interacting. Additionally when we feel something or have a moment of insightful thought, these thoughts / impulses register as energy on a variety of inner levels.

Generally science has taught us physical stimuli are felt in our body and mind (consciousness). For example, pain is felt where the skin is pierced and registers in our mind; when injured, our whole being fills with a burning, tearing sensation. Similarly emotions register in our body and consciousness. Our science has proven, chemically, tears of sorrow are different than tears of joy. Yes, emotions and thoughts have a chemical formula to them.

According to the mystic, all consciousness originates and begins in the soul. We are spiritual beings and this is our lasting self (aspect). When the physical body decays, our consciousness will journey on.

The soul has both a higher and lower center; these centers coincide with various stimuli. Higher stimuli, for example, are spiritual impulses to help others and lower stimuli are selfish thoughts which exceed our daily physical needs.

One who is able to act along with the higher impulse has become master of self and the microcosm; and because the microcosm is now aligned, through this process, with the macrocosm, the traveler is said to be master of all three dimensions.

# 36. What is the nature of the spiritual journey? What is its outcome?

Consider a drop of water, in its journey to the sea, and it undergoes change.

One day the drop is mist. The next it has become part of a passing cloud. On the third day, the drop falls onto the ground as a raindrop; eventually the drop seeps down into the earth and joins other drops as part of a mountain stream. Eventually this stream winds its way into a river and the river empties, along with the drop, into a mighty ocean.

Now this drop of water as it lies in the ground may be frozen for a time and in the spring thaw join as part of a lovely flower. In time the moisture in the flower evaporates back into the air and the drop, again, becomes part of a passing cloud. However, in this next cycle, it falls on the earth as part of a winter snow. Eventually the drop melts and seeps into the ground. Gradually it resumes the journey of finding its way to the mountain stream, river and ocean.

Throughout the journey, the drop changes many times, assumes different roles and learns about itself in a variety of ways. When it joins the ocean, the drop will be that much more complete and conscious of its potential. It is always a drop of water.

In part this is the nature of the soul's journey through the many worlds. One of the differences between our journey as humans is that we are able to show many more physical changes and manifestations of ourselves. However, the outcome our souls still seek to be complete and reach their highest potential through the many changes we experience.

## 37. Why must we die?

This is a question that has stirred philosophers throughout the ages; much has been written on this subject and this is an issue everyone faces.

The answer to this question can only be answered within the framework of your belief, philosophy and religious system. For example, if you are an agnostic, someone who does not believe in God, your answer to this question might be, there is nothing after the physical death. All we have is this life. Or if you believe in reincarnation, your answer will be, after the physical death, there is a period of evaluation of our life, then, according to different factors we move on to a higher plane or reenter the earth phase for another incarnation.

Because death is a reality for everyone, during the course of his or her life, it is something which requires attention. Each person must come to some answer about this event and reconcile the fear attached.

Remember, from our frame of reference it is possible for different beliefs to be true; depending from which level of reality they are viewed. Certainly, at this level of reality the agnostic's view is true; however, what is the view from the seventh heaven?

It is important to remember that all philosophical systems about the mystery of life must incorporate death into their framework. On one level, the natural outcome of life is death of the physical body. Basically we cannot get around this issue and must come to some conclusion about it. Our answer might be, "well I'll just wait and see what happens." However incomplete this might be for some, it is still an answer.

From a mystical view, death is a change into another form of existence, a more complete, spiritual existence. The goal of the mystical process is to incorporate the spiritual into daily life; the mystic wishes to operate from both dimensions while in the physical body and make this dual reality a part of ordinary consciousness. Since our lasting nature, according to the mystic, is spiritual and we entered the earth phase to advance in spiritual learning, the mystic wishes to do the work of the next phase, in this phase.

So we die, because we were created to live and experience, then change into something else. Like the caterpillar, we are in the process of building our cocoon and preparing for life as a butterfly.

Yesterday you were a caterpillar,
Today you are a butterfly.
Tomorrow what will you become?

## 38. I am frightened please tell me something to help ease my fear. Why must the physical body decay and die?

In death the reason for life is more visible. Death of the physical body is necessary for a vital lesson to be learned. The universe is in motion, constantly changing, connected by energy, recreating itself according to various designs. This is our destiny as well.

To the poet, life is like an afternoon at the shore. The sunlight, ocean spray, sand and multitude of sea creatures are to be enjoyed. We come for a few hours, experience the many sensations with family and friends, then return renewed to our other duties in life.

As we rest and watch the motion of the ocean waves, they remind us of our lasting nature. We are children of spirit who came into this realm to enjoy the afternoon's experience, learn, work, serve and move on. Death of the physical body is necessary so the spiritual lesson is learned; our lasting nature is spirit and like the universe, after the physical death we continue to evolve.

The body is a wonder of nature and evolution, yet, derives its driving force from spirit. This magnificent, efficient, and highly complex organism is created, has work to do, then returns to the elements from which it came. This cycle exists to remind us of our relationship with the Divine. We are here for an enjoyable afternoon, to do our work and then move on.

In time, the sting of death is replaced with the peace of acceptance and knowledge that we are children of spirit. And our lasting destiny is to dance across the stars.

# 39. What is the truth about heaven and hell?

The picture of heaven and hell that has been placed in your mind is a creation of man. The afterlife with angels and devils is not like this.

For the most part this vision is a social construct and has been placed in your mind by others for selfish ends. Behaviors of populations, to achieve specific outcomes needed by political leaders and religious teachers, are more easily controlled when people are frightened. Particularly when populations believe directives are coming from God through religious representatives. Think about how, in everyday life, if you become afraid of something or something suddenly scares you, you freeze like a "deer in headlights." This is the same dynamic that is at work when we talk about the construct of heaven and hell as it has been presented to us.

While there are serious consequences for actions that harm self and others, these outcomes are not simply burning in hell for evil doers and clouds with angels for the righteous. People must take responsibility for their lives and learn what is most helpful for their own development. They learn this by following a spiritual path and gradually learning to hear their own inner wisdom.

Remember you are a child of Light (God) and have come into this realm to work, love and serve by drawing closer to the Light. Certain actions bring you closer and certain actions distance you. Learn to follow the higher impulse which already exists deep within you. Then scenarios painted by others of heaven and hell will no longer confuse you.

## 40. Do souls come back or reincarnate?

This is another teaching which in its popularized version has been simplified. There is a reality and, in the past, a version of this reality was used by governments and religious institutions to further their own purpose.

In the Bible, which many consider to be holy, there is mention of great souls like Elijah incarnating or returning. Many religious systems acknowledge this potential. Inside each of us, there is a part that does not die when the body dies. Different belief systems call this part the soul, spirit or heart. Whatever name you use, this is the part we are discussing and will carry us to the next world.

However, the question remains, does every soul reincarnate and to what purpose? Also are the 'bad' things that happen due to karma and past behavior?

In answering this question, one must take into account there is a real possibility that aspects of what you learned about spirituality and religion are incomplete. The teachings of your youth, no matter how well intended, may not have taken into account the factor of belief and the possibility of different things being true at the same time.

In order to answer the question about reincarnation, you have to push aside for a moment your preconceptions and consider that reincarnation exists and it may not be like what you were taught. So, what is the reality? Consider this possibility. Each soul journeys through the universe and experiences, loves, works and serves. The point of the multi-level existence is to return to the Creator that much more complete and serve in kingship. Each can be a king and creator within their own world. That is the souls' potential.

In this realm, there are countless opportunities to experience the many levels of spiritual potential. Here we can begin to experience our ultimate spiritual destiny; this is a very special place. With respect to this life, each soul decides what it is to learn and with whom it wishes to learn these things. Then according to the higher law and destiny of the universe, souls incarnate. This world is a vast classroom and we come to work and learn together. So yes, reincarnation exists.

# 41. Is there anything more I should know about reincarnation? People often talk about what's possible "When I come back in my next life…" Is this something that is actually possible? A soul contemplating the next lessons to be learned when it returns to the earth?

Because much has been written about this aspect and much has been proliferated as a control mechanism, we will discuss those issues most pertinent to our present work. However before beginning, it is important to keep in mind, that in some societies, this teaching was used and is used as a method to control a population by declaring something like. "People must be content with their present status because it is what they earned and in future lives they have unlimited potential and can gain in material benefits."

We must remember, the use of a religious teaching by a social institution to control a population is nothing new and goes on all around us, every day. Part of the purpose of the present work is to help point out some conditions under which this occurs and offer the reader another direction. Also, the reader must keep in mind that rules of a religious teaching have positive aspects as well. One of the purposes of organized religion is to provide a social structure and healthy ordering of our lives.

From the mystical frame of reference, reincarnation is accepted by many. We were born, and came into the earth phase to learn and advance. Then after completing this learning, we move on into something else. This something else is spiritual and may involve going over what we have learned and making a decision, in accord with the higher elements and the higher destiny of the universe, about the next phase. This may or may not involve reentering the earth phase.

This process may be repeated many times or something else might occur, depending upon individual destiny. Everything, however, from the soul's perspective is seen from the present moment. So, at this time, there may or may not be planning concerning which lessons are to be addressed in the next phase.

The final destination, however, is to merge with the

Absolute and return completed; to assume our role as the son / daughter of a King.

Depending upon the religious context, all souls incarnate or move from one spiritual reality to another. Also most religions accept that great souls return to the earth phase to help others reach higher; the monotheisms acknowledge this aspect as well. Presently, those who follow specific monotheistic teachings are awaiting the return of the Messiah.

However, according to mystical tradition, specific teachings about reincarnation were left out of the Bible. It is suggested, by some sources this was done to strengthen the role of the clergy. Further it is suggested, if the average person became more aware of their own latent spirituality, they might be less reliant upon others. Once again, this viewpoint is presented as an alternative to some of these common beliefs.

A popular view is that one can reincarnate even as a lower life form, if this is justified by one's actions. This is not accurate. Always we are evolving higher.

Note the following points about reincarnation:

- People reincarnate or come back to the earth phase as an improved version of them selves. In the spiritual realm, a decision is made about the next phase and may include a return to the earth phase. Souls are not forced to reincarnate, they must want to do this; remember we are spirits with free will.
- All souls incarnate into different, higher realms on the return journey back to the Absolute.
- The earth phase is a special place to learn and souls generally look forward to incarnating here. This phase is a place for many experiences and possibilities.

- Souls incarnate to learn specific lessons of which there are many or to validate learning in a specific area. Whether or not a soul is in a "change" or "validation" incarnation is independent of their present level of spirituality.
- Generally we do not remember our past lives because they would distract us, cause us pain or be a source of false pride. We bring with us into this incarnation what we need to make this journey. In this process, there is no punishment; we advance based upon our individual effort and the mercy of God.
- Each day we are reborn into a new life and have the opportunity to learn, change and move forward. People forget each day is a beginning.
- This process is intended as a blessing; not a punishment 'until we get it right.' Many of the laws that govern this process are hidden from us and are a mystery.
- We do get the choice, under certain parameters, as to the circumstances under which (sex, race and location) and with whom we wish to incarnate. Tradition has it there are four Masters of Reincarnation that help guide souls in this regard.
- In the cosmic journey, each soul is reaching higher to become the best version of self. It is the said that the return journey back to the Absolute, for many, begins in this earth realm
- For spiritual learning, the earth phase is a very special place. Because of the pull of the physical reality, a friction is created between the physical and spiritual. This friction increases the potential for spiritual learning.

## 42. Two concepts that go along with the discussion of reincarnation are the Law of Karma and the Law of Grace. Can you tell me more about these?

In the universe, there is a natural law that for every action there is an equal or opposite reaction.

Karma is the natural return of thoughts, actions and desires to their point of origin. Or put more simply, what we put out toward others returns to us, sometimes even with greater intensity.

One of the principles we must remember is that thoughts contain energy and we have to be aware of our thoughts and monitor them; thoughts when they leave us can develop into an elemental. This elemental, or thought form, seeks to attach itself to a conduit to make it happen and if this is not possible returns to us (usually) in a stronger version.

An example of how the energy of Karma works can be applied to the process of planning to go on vacation. As we anticipate this happy event, we picture ourselves swimming and playing in the sun and relaxing. This thought form, if strong enough, has a life of its own; it will seek to attach itself to a vehicle to be able to express itself. In this case, it attaches itself to circumstances, such as the time we can get off from work and when we can afford the plane ticket. These practical concerns along with the thought form influence our decision to go. We finally go on vacation to Miami Beach and realize our vision of swimming and playing in the sun. The elemental has served its function; however, if we do not go on the desired vacation, when the thought form / energy returns to us, it may help make us resentful around the circumstances that prevented us from going. Depending upon the situation, we hold resentment toward employer or spouse or flight carrier and if we keep replaying this tape in our head, resentment can turn into lasting emotional distress.

On one level this is the Law of Karma playing out. In the above scenario, thoughts have returned to us both positively and negatively. Usually, when people consider the Law of Karma they look only to visible action. For example, we do or say something harmful to another, thereby creating negative karma for us and later in the week our car breaks down. Immediately we connect the two events and believe, inaccurately, this is the law of karma in action, i.e., what we put out into the world, at some point returns to us and can be distasteful.

However, karma is a learning tool. Sometimes, the lessons can carry across lifetimes.

Let's get back to our vacation scenario, where the person does not get to go on vacation. Due to all of his expectations, he harbors resentment toward the one who denied his vacation and this resentment turns into anger. Over time, this anger festers, and leads to a depression or an act of overt aggression. Eventually, this person may seek treatment and learns, for the most part, he was the cause of his own problem. By continuing to expect something, instead of accepting a disappointing outcome and continuing to relive perceived harm, over and over in his head / consciousness, he created his own illness / negative circumstances

In psychological terms, this was an expectation cycle that grew into a depression or act of violence and once the patient learned his own part, he gradually was freed of the cycle by substituting healthier thoughts. In effect, our subject was cured from his own incorrect thinking and its consequences.

So, this person created an expectation, in a thought form, that returned to him. This thought form or elemental attached itself to his anger instead of attaching itself to his acceptance of the situation; this person could have created thoughts that accepted the situation. If the thought form had attached itself to acceptance that yes, the vacation was not possible this year, but possibly some other time the cycle would have been broken.

But because it attached itself to anger, the thought form grew and kept replaying itself, as he contemplated and repeated the harm that was done him, until it became a form of illness; anger turned inward in this scenario became depression or a delayed act of aggression.

On the other side of this, the Law of Grace states that through prayer and Divine Forgiveness we may be freed of past karma.

If we truly repent and ask Forgiveness, God is Most Merciful and will forgive karmic debt or as it is stated in some religious traditions, sins against self and others.

One mystical teaching describes Christ's role in absolving karmic debt. Christ died upon the Cross and took on the sins of the world; in this passing of pain and sorrow, Christ assumed the karmic debt of humanity; and people, through this act, were forever freed from their past, present, and future debt. When people sincerely repent and ask forgiveness, according to this teaching this is the potential result. Thus began a new age of spiritual absolution and forgiveness.

Further it is believed, karmic debt is played out through different bodily illnesses and difficult events in a person's life. Many religious traditions hold that certain individuals, because of their spiritual development, can assume the karmic debt or sins of others. This is an operant tradition of Christianity; and as the person sincerely repents, sins are forgiven and absolved because of the contract of the Cross.

However, for people of all traditions, the Law of Grace states; sincerely ask and make the effort to change and it shall be forgiven. God is all merciful.

# 43. Why aren't we consciously aware of our karmic debt to others?

Part of your task as a conscious being is to be aware of your actions toward others; you must awaken in yourself the ability to recognize when you have caused another pain, then go to them and ask for their forgiveness. Also, you must learn to avoid hurting others and initiating a situation where the energy that is produced is harmful.

It is spiritual law, that when you have harmed another, you must go to them and sincerely request their forgiveness. Even if they refuse, if the request is sincere, this action / energy dissolves your debt. Additionally, because of their refusal, the person may create a situation where they add to their own debt.

We are not consciously aware of karmic debt carried across incarnations for two reasons. First, this awareness would be harmful, psychologically, in the present life and serve as a distraction. Secondly, the Law of Grace absolves much of this debt. While preparing for the next incarnation and going over the events of the past life, if the soul sincerely repents and asks God for forgiveness, much of this debt is removed.

## 44. How do we get to work out karma with other people across incarnations?

One of the choices the soul has before entering the earth phase is with whom they would like to work their life-plan. It is important to remember that while we journey as an individual, we also journey as a member of humanity. Originally, when we were created and entered the physical universe and came through the Idea of Man, we entered both as an individual and with others. These are our kindred spirits, with whom we vibrate similarly. As fate dictates, we work with these people, whom we instantly recognize, in different situations throughout our lives.

The interrelationship of karma between different people in our lives is far too complicated to explain and understand. This relationship is monitored and controlled by the Masters of Reincarnation and their helpers.

If you are concerned about your karmic debt and how you affect others, there are actions you can take. Daily, you can monitor your thoughts and how you treat others; if you have injured another, sincerely repent and ask for their forgiveness. Then, as God Wills, the Law of Grace will set you free from your past actions (sins).

# 45. What is the point of religious teaching, if some organized religion has caused us to be so in doubt as to our true spiritual purpose?

The original teachers, who are credited with founding the great religions, came here to teach people about the ultimate nature of reality and provide a ladder upon which people could climb to reach their higher, spiritual potential. The followers who wished to offer these wonderful teachings to a wider audience, created a structure to do this.

Over time and with the influence of different people, some with selfish motives, individual teachings were altered, and now exist in a manipulated form. Also we must remember teachings were offered to specific people at a specific time; hence the teaching takes into account the personality, or frame of reference, of a specific audience. Not all teachings automatically translate to all people at all times. That is why teachings are updated. Teachings are kept vibrant by living teachers and are specific to their present audience.

Religious teaching, for most people, provides a structure from which spiritual learning can occur. The student is taught about their soul / spirit and how to be a better person. This is a starting point. However, for many, they remain fixed at this level. And, as we have seen throughout history, politicians and heads of religious organizations can use religious teaching negatively as a manipulative tool.

A point often not made clear enough is that there is both an internal and external reality to religious experience. Externally a teaching is subject to limitations of time, place and even distortion; however, internally the spiritual reality is vibrant and in tune with the Divine.

On a deep level, all religious teaching is unified; religions differ externally. Internally, the great religions are One and transcendent.

Until recently, the emphasis has been on externals. These are the outward things that you do – attend mass, say your rosary, go to the temple, etc. Some religions have neglected to teach the deep, inner worship. That is the reason for the groundswell in exotic and different spiritual paths, and perhaps why you are coming to question things now. There is an inner hunger in the masses.

For many travelers, the great religions provide a structure from which spiritual learning grows. Through a specific presentation, the traveler is taught about their soul and spirit; and how to become a better person. This learning provides a basis for life and a starting point for deeper study. However many travelers cannot see beyond their own individual learning structure, and are slow to accept this and other structures work for different travelers. We all learn through different methods.

Externally a teaching is subject to individuality with limitations of time, place and even decay; yet internally the spiritual reality is vibrant and One with the Absolute. Across time and space the great religions are transcendent.

Since the beginning, religious differences have been used as a way to exert one group's will against another. While we are on the spiritual path of learning, we will begin to see the differences in teaching for manipulation and teaching for true spiritual growth.

## 46. What purpose does organized religion as we know it serve?

Religion is a structure through which spiritual learning can begin. As the traveler advances, spiritual learning may take place outside of a religious context. Spiritual experience is the natural extension of religious inquiry; the great religions were created to be vehicles, for people to start learning about them selves and their relationship with Truth.

The followers of a great teacher or Prophet, in order to help spread the teaching, created a system to do this. Often the Prophet did not create many of the elements that combined to form a religion; the Prophet presented the current method to perceive and align with Truth.

One of the tendencies of the earth phase is repetition; repetition is a helpful tool in most forms of learning. Generally, religious teaching makes good use of this; however, repetition has a tendency to lead toward hardening. This hardening or fossilization, slowly, replaces the living or vibrant element. In recent years, this lack of vibrancy has caused some to turn away from religion and seek spiritual experience elsewhere.

It is important for everyone to have a basic spiritual grounding and in our culture this happens in religious training and worship. This is a starting place and because this learning is intended to be enriched and built upon, often it is basic and designed to reach large numbers of people. As the child matures from this foundation, other forms of spiritual experience become possible.

While it is possible to have advanced spiritual learning and experience within the context of organized religion, this form of learning is not emphasized and generally not acknowledged to be available. Due to this lack of emphasis, people seek this experience elsewhere.

To make this clearer, let us take the example of carpentry. When the apprentice carpenter is first learning his / her trade, they are given the most basic of tasks, often these are repetitious, but gradually the apprentice learns about wood, and its many uses. After a period of training, working on a number of projects, and interacting with other trades, the apprentice graduates into becoming a carpenter.

As the years pass, and the carpenter seeks to increase learning, he studies how trees grow and effects environmental conditions have upon grade, its elasticity and longevity. In time, he may become adept at knowing how the wood will weather, and if it will last, simply by its smell and feel.

As he reaches middle years, the carpenter continues learning and works on projects in the city and country. Over the years, he has worked with wood, in his region, in every conceivable fashion. Compared to the basic, repetitious education of the young apprentice, our mature carpenter in this way became a master.

## 47. Why does God allow so much suffering and destruction in the world? Why are tyrants and psychopaths free to destroy?

Man / woman was created with free will and the earth phase is a place for learning. Man creates much of the disharmony, fear and pain in the world. Similarly man can create happiness, beauty, and for the most part, elimination of fear. That is the potential and humanity is evolving to a higher condition. That is the Plan and its completion is far in the future. Yet each soul can reach this potential, individually and in this lifetime.

You wonder why evil men and tyrants exist. At present they are part of the earth phase and individually choose their path. Similarly others have the capacity to resist, stop them and create a better world. In these actions, there is much learning and opportunity for souls to grow and advance. How much more are we able to learn when we can see all the differences that are possible in the expression of the soul? If we were all the same, all the time, how would we know that there are other possibilities?

We learn as much from the expression of evil as we do from the expression of goodness.

## 48. So if all this is true, and I have a real destiny in terms of my soul, how does free will choice fit into things?

In earlier times, religion taught that man had free will and was destined to use this ability for the greater good and to do God's work. This quality separated man from other creatures and was indicative of man's special spiritual rank.

The present formulation of the teaching is much the same; however, due to cultural differences and scientific emphasis, minor adjustments are required.

Man is conscious and for the most part freely creates what he thinks, feels and how he spends the day. Most traditions offer that the plight of the common person is 'sleep;' and only those 'enlightened' ones are truly awake, and capable of making real choice.

Further there is an aspect to man, a life giving energy, which seems to be present in all other things. When this energy and man's consciousness are aligned, everyone benefits and man can purposively fulfill his or her higher spiritual destiny by exerting his or her free will.

The other way to look at this is much like a trail in the woods. Usually, if we come across a trail, there are several little paths that take off from the main trail and show us different things in the woods. This is part of the fun, but it can also get us lost. In order to get to the end of the trail, all paths must eventually bring us back to the center. Our final destination remains the same. We just make different choices on how to get there!

## 49. Are some things bad and others good?

In our age, we have learned that some behaviors, habits and desires can be destructive to the individual. However these same behaviors when in moderation may be beneficial.

Scientifically we have discovered that while one glass of wine at dinner, for most people, is relaxing and even medicinal, for others it sets off alcoholic and destructive behaviors. In this case, the wine is neither bad nor good. It is its effect upon the person that is the operant factor. Similarly while one piece of cake after dinner is enjoyable, having cake after every dinner, depending upon metabolism and exercise might lead to a problem with weight or cholesterol.

For most situations, people simplify and use the rule: everything in moderation. While this works for many things, it does not work for everything. Is a moderate amount of war or terrorism acceptable? Certainly this statement can stir up lengthy and heated discussions. But it is a good guideline for a lot of things.

In the spiritual realm, behavior, events and desires are viewed as learning experiences. Value judgments are pushed aside and the determining factor, in evaluating experience, is whether or not we learned something that helped us reach toward our higher nature and completion. Everything has the potential to be a spiritual lesson.

## 50. What is the learning we are to accomplish? Is it one major lesson and then we have mastered the meaning of life or is there more to it?

In answering this question, let us consider an example from everyday life.

A youngster goes to school to acquire learning necessary to live and prosper in the world. In each subject area, there are many lessons. While the overall lesson, or reason to attend school, is acquisition of skills to live in the world, each subject area has an endless depth of learning.

Similarly the spiritual traveler enters the earth phase to learn, work, love and serve. Yet within each of these areas is varied experience and learning.

In this endeavor, the outcome is the complete person, who is aligned spiritually, mentally, emotionally, and physically with his/her own destiny and the higher destiny of the universe. When this alignment is complete the person is the master of his/her own kingdom. This evolutionary process exists because each person has a higher function to complete.

The point of all of this teaching and learning along life's path is to produce the complete human being; a traveler who is in tune with the Source, participates in the everyday world and consciously serves the Higher Will. That is the "big lesson."

Each traveler is created with a wide range of talents and interests; the point of this life is to express these abilities in the world and do this as a servant of the

Light. We were not created to go off someplace, live the life of a recluse and contemplate our navel – what would happen if we all did that?

The world needs more travelers who are in tune with the many aspects of themselves and work to make this world a better place. This is the multi-dimensional part of what we're learning in life. Some do this working for a big corporation others do this daily in their role as parents. Still others are visibly operating as advocates for the less fortunate. Each has something to offer the world and this world benefits when each works together and submits to the Light.

# 51. In today's world, many are turning to drugs, sex and self-indulgent behavior. Why are people so destructive?

Each of us has an excitement need and the world is a giant bazaar with many exciting opportunities. Also each of us is born with an inner spiritual emptiness, or void, which needs to be filled. Many become confused and spend significant portions of their life seeking the missing piece in potentially harmful areas.

There is a difference between casual experimentation and learning, and destructive, habitual use. To a large extent, segments of our society have glamorized and made fashionable indulging the senses and individual desires. These elements use other people's excitement need and exploit it for gain.

For many, religion has gotten old, lost its capacity

to excite and help, and motivates only through fear. Sadly people turn away from this essential element and look to ease their inner hunger elsewhere. Yet religion, or spiritual capacity, is intended to be the center; the point from which a life develops. It is the missing piece, and at its highest level, fills the inner hunger, gives meaning, direction, excitement and energy to life. Sadly, the inner hunger can never be filled by these other addictive activities.

## 52. Why do some people remain in the darkness or depression for extended periods and not try to reach toward the Light?

Each soul enters the earth phase to grow closer toward the Light. Just as the daylight follows the night, so, in each life there comes opportunity to embrace the object of the search. This cycle of darkness and Light is part of the journey.

Fear and the need for structure contribute to people's resistance to change. While uncomfortable, they are frightened to reach and pull themselves out of the darkness. These people require assistance, and as God Wills, aid arrives in many forms.

## 53. What of the one that is harmed or killed in this process? What about them?

We are more than flesh. We are beings of consciousness and spirit. When the body dies, is that the end of existence? In a death that is painful, it is difficult but we must think, "What does the soul learn?" Perhaps in this sort of death and the surrounding circumstance, it was the only way the lesson could be learned.

Remember each soul must taste the sting of death. This realm is one form of existence. One of the great ones has said our journey through this life is like a horse rider, who stops to rest beneath a shady tree, finds some refreshment and then travels on.

There is an existence after we pass through this life and a painful death may be essential to the next phase.

## 54. What is the effect of people lying, cheating and stealing?

Besides the obvious effect upon the person who has been taken advantage of there is an effect upon people who learn about this activity, and an effect on the person who commits the transgression. Some of the effects are long term and others more immediate.

In all action, there is energy that is created and this energy requires a conduit; as it attaches to a conduit and manifests in the physical realm, there may be physical and psychological consequences of harmful events. The Law of Karma and a world full of elementals, seeking a conduit, can create a negative and disturbing vibration. In part, this is what occurs when news sources keep reporting and showing painful events. The thought forms they recreate contribute to an environment that is negatively charged and makes people further anxious.

People are responsible for their actions and the energy they think and create. On some level, all of this energy must be dissipated and used. Unless the person sincerely repents, invoking the Law of Grace, at some point, they will have to face their own potentially harmful energy.

## 55. Why can't learning be less painful? Can't we learn in another way?

Perhaps the lesson was presented many times, unsuccessfully, in other less disturbing ways. In this matter, much is hidden from us and we have to accept the possibility that a painful passing might be the most effective way to teach the lesson.

For Christianity, consider the traditional account of Christ's death upon the cross; how would the lesson of Christ's life have altered if he died, old and infirm in his bed? If he passed in a less compelling fashion, certainly, the impact of his death and life might have changed their history.

God knows what each soul needs. In this matter, we have to trust in something higher than ourselves. If we are open, and truly submit ourselves to the higher purpose of the spiritual path, lessons can be more easily learned.

## 56. What is a miracle? How do they occur?

A miracle is an event that is outside normal, everyday activity and appears to transcend the natural physical laws. Often it involves the participation of a teacher / traveler who facilitates, or causes the event through inner spiritual cognition. Usually it is in a religious or spiritual learning framework. The activity requires the interplay of Truth or God, and the event raises belief, learning, and serves as evidence of a Higher Law.

One of the great spiritual teachers, when questioned about miracles, replied that they are actions upon the natural, physical law; are in harmony with the potential of the situation and in accord with the higher destiny. There is nothing miraculous about them. The catalyst / person through inner capacity brings about a potential latent in the situation. Ultimately, the outcome is aligned with Truth and the point most often is a lesson to the larger community. Miracles work on many levels; their potential is cumulative and they affect many travelers.

In the biblical account of Jesus raising Lazarus from the dead, consider who was affected by this event and in how many ways. Someone who was dead is now alive; also, Lazarus' family is overjoyed, witnesses are stunned and 2000 years later we are still wondering at the possibility that this actually occurred. How many have gained significant knowledge from this one "miracle?"

Or, consider the birth of a child. Science explains this phenomenon as the fertilization of an egg by a sperm. The mysterious piece or the part that is not yet understood is how the life force energy presents itself and a living embryo is created. It is at this point science, religion and spiritual laws interact. Clearly, in this activity, there is the coming together of natural phenomena that we partially understand and spiritual laws that we do not. Part of the process remains unclear and some term this lack of understanding miraculous.

Both in mythology and religious history, there is reference to virgin births. On occasion great souls are born without benefit of sexual activity. In these accounts it is asserted the life force, in some unknown way, acts upon the egg and an embryo develops. Clearly, this is outside our scientific understanding and believers trust their belief system and accept this account. The point of a miraculous or virgin birth is to raise spiritual consciousness.

According to great spiritual teachers, miracles are a byproduct of a higher state of consciousness. They are organic actions that use spiritual and physical laws to bring about an extraordinary event. They happen because it is a natural, latent potential, and the teacher intuitively senses and facilitates this action to bring about the event.

Because miracles are organic and arise out of the potential in a situation, travelers cannot be taught how to perform them. Spiritually, the teacher / traveler perceives a potential, acts upon the situation in accord with a higher design, something seemingly miraculous occurs. Consistently, the teacher / traveler insists this event is the byproduct of the situation's potential and natural laws.

Practitioners of magic, to cause actions, learn to use natural physical laws. These actions involve the practitioner's will (desire), and the use of physical laws and intention. In this case, the outcome comes about as a result of the magician's *desire to cause* and the result is illusory (more temporary). In magic, the action occurs at a lower physical level and is not aligned with Ultimate Truth. It is tradition that magicians never prosper, because their activity involves their own desire, natural laws and an extension of personal will; not the Will of Ultimate Truth.

Hence we see in the Koran, the story of Moses and the Magicians. When Pharaoh Commands a contest by throwing down staffs (walking sticks), Moses' staff turns into a larger serpent and consumes all the smaller snakes (from the other Magician's staffs). Immediately, due to fear, the Magicians bow down to Moses and his higher magic (Divine Will); even at the risk of their lives. Bowing down to Moses makes the Pharaoh angry and he threatens to kill all the court Magicians. In this event, the Divine Will was expressed through magic because at the time this was more easily understood by the masses.

## 57. How will the shift to universal higher consciousness occur?

We are in the beginning of it. Look around and notice the increasing interest in different religious philosophies and how so many are returning to the faith of their childhood. See the general discontent in the way government is being run and the growing awareness that republicans or democrats cannot save us. From the outside, our way of life is being attacked by those who want to return to a more traditional and religious based social system (as defined by them). It is generally recognized that greed in the marketplace is destroying our middle class. The family fabric is being strained with couples having to work three jobs. Soon we will be a society of rich and poor.

Many are beginning to wonder, what went wrong? Also many are searching for answers.

We are living in an age when people are turning away from authority-based to individual-based action. Over time many realized we have given up too much responsibility to authority and institutions; gradually people are taking back control of their lives.

The shift has occurred and will continue. Remember that a better world is created one person at a time. It took a long time to get to the point that society is at right now. It will take a long time to bring us to a better world then, too.

In order to create better people, we have to add the missing ingredient. This enriching element balances individual greed and helps the individual realize, because of our complex world, often our best interest is served looking out for others. For example, we may have to spend money to upgrade the air filtering capacity of our car engine; so, we have clean air to breathe. This may cost personally, but in the long run our air quality is healthier.

According to the mystic, the missing ingredient and balancing factor is higher consciousness. This consciousness, because of its alignment with Truth, enables the individual to work toward collective interest. This potential is latent in everyone, and its individual development and operation will save us and we can continue with our evolution.

This is a new frontier and area of inquiry. How can each develop inner wisdom and higher consciousness? How can each become a wise man / woman and achieve excellence in their daily life?

There is a way to do this, but we have forgotten where and how to look. The next phase will see its reemergence. The process begins with the type of questioning that people are engaging in now.

## 58. How do I go about finding the "missing ingredient?"

Turn back to the religion of your youth; become a better Christian, Jew or Moslem. Seek the inner core of religious experience and do not be satisfied with the teachings of others. Find your own inner Truth and become a spiritual traveler. Each of the great religions provides a structure or framework from which to begin the inner journey of exploration of self and higher consciousness.

If for some reason your journey is restricted by the religion of your birth, seek Truth and higher consciousness in another spiritual path. Pray and ask for a different way to open to you. Pray for a guide and teacher who will show you your own inner potential and teach awareness of your growing spirituality. Find a teacher that is aligned with Truth and will give you tools to uncover your own strength, and teach you how to proceed on your own.

In this endeavor, three factors must be aligned: the student, the teacher and the grace (Baraka) of the path.

It is tradition that the teacher calls to the student's

sincerity or purity of heart; this is the factor that enables the student to be successful. How do you grow sincere in your efforts? Seek Truth or wisdom for its own sake not for what it will give you. Seek Truth because you love and must know it. Then, as God Wills, the golden or inner path will open to you.

This is the missing ingredient. One day this awareness will be as common as your knowing that the sun will come up in the morning.

## 59. Until I achieve this inner understanding, what should I do?

Try to live a good, balanced life. Achieve excellence in something. Seek to help others and develop the many aspects of yourself. Make time to listen to your inner song. Stay away from that which is destructive. Do things in moderation and try not to hurt people. Be kind to yourself and others. Be a good loving person that is an asset to their family, community and world.

## 60. All this sounds like 'do gooder' stuff. How do I know this is not just another religion looking for followers? How do I know this is the "real" right answer for me?

Life is both simple and complex. Internally most people know when they are doing something that will harm themselves or another. The problem is they cannot break free of the destructive pattern. If you wish to change, turn inward, pray and ask for help. Also try to follow the path described above. In time, if you are sincere, a door will open to you.

However if you are content with your life, then, stay as you are. Also, if another path, with different promises and instructions appeals to you, follow it. You see, in this matter, you are free to pick and choose. Keep in mind you have to be careful not to cause lasting harm to yourself or another. Yet you can try as many things as you like until it feels right.

# 61. Can two things, seemingly different, be true at the same time?

Yes. Have you ever gotten into a discussion with your significant other where both were at polar opposites? For example one wishes to paint the house and the other does not. In this situation, we are not considering if the house needs paint, to what degree and by which standard but simply if the people involved want it painted. In this scenario there is no correct answer and in time a compromise is reached, one gives into another or the matter remains unresolved.

Now one of the characteristics of indoctrination systems, is they foster particular beliefs and offer others who disagree are incorrect. Each will claim that they are "really right." This type of belief system is rigid with little room for difference and is the most difficult to engage in compromise. Examples of indoctrination systems exist within political, religious and extremist groups. Followers of indoctrination systems often oppose anyone who does not believe similarly.

One might think that indoctrinated people are single minded extremists and maybe a bit crazy. Therefore due to their beliefs, it would be easy to recognize, discount or even marginalize them. However, this is not always so, because sometimes we are the indoctrinated. What makes indoctrination so insidious is that we are often unaware of our own intolerance, prejudice, feelings of privilege and dogmatism.

Now let us turn for a moment to specific religious or spiritual beliefs. For example, does reincarnation exist or not? People's beliefs, opinions and religious doctrines are all over the place on this. Some religions claim reincarnation is true and others do not. Additionally, some religions state specific circumstances under which it occurs and many details. Yet, to someone of another faith, this is not a central issue and according to his or her belief system, reincarnation does not exist.

Well, which view is correct? As with our example: about painting the house, perhaps both or neither? Also in this matter we must consider the energy produced by believing and the effect it has upon reality. In the medical field, doctors and other healers are becoming aware people who believe they are going to get well have a greater chance of recovering from serious illness. The energy around belief, in part, leads to recovery.

Or perhaps there is a dimension, or energy engendered by belief, when attached to a possibility serves as a catalyst and causes things to occur.

The universe is a vast place and it is possible for all kinds of things to be true simultaneously. This is perhaps one of the hardest things to accept, but if you look closely in your day to day life, you will see that this shows itself to be true in numerous ways.

Now one person believes there is a God and another does not. Are both correct? On one level: yes. On the level of personal belief and experience both are correct. Yet ultimately, in the larger universe, only one is accurate.

It is possible for people to believe things that are not true for others and in time, it is possible for them to accept something else. People believe and accept at the level to which they are most comfortable. Also it is possible for people to believe something and cause it to happen. The individual, who goes around believing they are accident prone, creates a state of consciousness that helps pull mishaps toward them. Then others start observing, "Boy, she is really accident prone." And the belief of others starts to make that state of consciousness even stronger. So more accidents happen!

# 62. Why do bad things happen? Particularly to people who try to live good lives?

One of the physical laws of the universe is that flesh is subject to deterioration, injury and death. Pain, illness and fluctuation of emotion are part of the way we were created; our biological, physiological and emotional interplay is part of our evolutionary design.

Additionally, two of our mental characteristics, a tendency to compare things and have expectations from others, often lead to emotional pain. The comparison and expectation cycle mentally helps to set up disappointment. The mind questions, "Why can't I be as smart as so and so or I have worked hard and should have gotten that promotion."

Instead of trying to accept our feelings of disappointment or work harder for the next opportunity, we have a tendency to internalize and blame ourselves or we tend to compare the circumstances of our lives to what is happening in other people's lives.

Consequently we play the tape in our minds, "I am not as smart as so and so and did not get the promotion because I am 'less than' him and bad things always happen to me." This negative thinking is counterproductive, feeds into a defeatist attitude, which in turn may subconsciously lead toward other failures. Instead of open and accepting self-talk, we generate negative energy that interacts upon future situations. Then our self-talk has a good chance of becoming a self-fulfilling prophecy.

On a spiritual and inner level, things that happen to us are neither bad nor good. They are learning opportunities, having the potential to teach us about our higher nature, help us move forward and learn about our place in the universe.

Some of the most difficult lessons are learned only under the most painful of circumstances. Most often, the lesson was not learned earlier, in a less stressful way and had to play out painfully.

Consider the lesson of one who has come into this life, in part, to learn about accepting help from others. Time after time, they refused assistance, stubbornly, rejecting help, insisting they can handle situations. In time this stubbornness contributed to a painful illness that resulted in death. Yet pain and illness may have been averted if the individual accepted aid from family and doctors. In this situation, because of past refusals and continuing stubbornness, only at the point of a painful and prolonged death could this person learn; sometimes we have to accept help from others.

# 63. Many times we are faced with decisions and do not know if an action will turn out positive or negative. Can you suggest a criteria or measuring stick that is useful?

When you first start out on the Path, knowing what to do is a daily concern. Usually, during the day we are faced with many opportunities that require a decision and often we are unsure. Repeatedly, we ask the question, will I benefit or will I lose?

As previously discussed, from a spiritual perspective all action and experience is a learning opportunity. Sometimes it is only by 'dancing across the flame' do we learn the lesson, however, in the interests of efficiency and wanting to minimize potentially painful decisions let me suggest the following criteria: If an action will bring you closer to your higher self then pursue it. If it will distance you then let it go.

Since none of us is born with a 'crystal ball' that tells us the outcome of things; we have to rely upon our decision-making skills. In this regard, let us examine a few facts. First, the everyday consciousness is not adept at making complex decisions; it works well with decisions that deal with comparison and logic.

However, in the area of more complex matters, situations that involve emotions, such as life-purpose or romance, you have to rely upon intuition. Inside each of us is a capacity to intuitively know things and we have to learn how to switch to this mode of thought. Some people call this using our 'gut' instinct and the more we do this the easier it becomes.

Before making a complex decision, ask your higher self, will this decision bring me closer to the Light or distance me? Then, turn inward and work with the answers. The criterion is movement toward Truth. If we are moving closer, then it is correct.

## 64. Are some things dark and evil? Is there a devil?

In each day, there is darkness and Light. In each heart there is capacity to move into the sunlight. The further we move from Truth, the darker our thoughts; the more we seek to help others, because our actions are aligned with Truth, our thoughts fill with Light.

Are there people whose actions are aligned with darkness? Yes. Are there people whose actions are aligned with Light? Yes. Remember on the highest planes there is no darkness only Light. The existence of darkness on the lower planes is there as something to learn from.

There are thought forms or energy patterns that vibrate at lower levels; these thought forms are dark and are created from anger, negativity and the desire to selfishly control and hurt. This conscious energy exists and interacts upon the situation creating darkness, pain and separation. We call this energy pattern evil.

The devil that has horns, red skin and is commonly pictured in movies or print is a composite and for the most part imagination. There is a dark essence, however, not in this form.

If you are faced with consciousness or energy that is frightening, say a prayer and turn toward the Light. Ask the Light to protect you and, as God Wills, you will be bathed in sunshine.

# 65. How do I balance the physical, mental and spiritual in my day-to-day living?

In order to live a complete life, a life that is tuned to your higher destiny, you must participate in the world and, at times, spiritually withdraw. Each person is created with a multitude of talents, emotions, hopes and dreams. Each person is an ocean with vast depths of undiscovered marine life, organisms, valleys, peaks and wrecked ships with treasure. All of these capacities, with training and opportunity have the potential for expression.

The key to a balanced life is moderation, expression of the many parts of self and following a spiritual path to completion. We came into the earth phase to do and be many things. A balanced life is working in the world, sharing a family, contributing to the benefit of others, seeing each day as an opportunity to grow closer to your lasting self, and serving Truth.

Daily set aside a few moments to center yourself and listen to your own inner song. If you wish pray, meditate, send healing energy to others, or ask Truth to guide your life. Inside is a golden potential that unlocks limitless energy and guards a hidden treasure.

- Everything in moderation, this is a general rule that many ignore. Extremes are to be avoided. Even too much spiritual activity can destroy your balance.
- Keep your conscious mind and thoughts focused on Truth. Thoughts are energy and return to us, and negative thoughts return many times over.
- 'Work in the world, but be not of it.' Have a job and support your family but keep a part of yourself apart. This is your sacred center; enter it to draw guidance and life-giving energy.
- In the morning and evening, set aside a few moments to honor that which gave us life and ask for guidance to make our life the living prayer.
- When problems are placed before you, 'remember problems exist so you can solve them.' Have a positive attitude, work hard and ask Truth for guidance.
- Honor your body and its emotions. Take the time to exercise, love, eat correctly, and express your feelings, moderately. These are essential aspects to the earth phase.
- Be generous and kind to others. Our good work returns to us as positive energy that raises us higher.

We are entering the age of self and leaving the age of authority. The solutions to the problems of this age are to be found within people, not institutions. While institutions may help, the solutions are waiting within each soul. Now our task is to develop better people who are closely aligned with Truth and work to solve the problems around us. Remember we are a wondrous creation that has forgotten how to use its magic wand.

## 66. How do the mind, body and spirit work together?

Spiritually we are a complex entity that simultaneously exists on three planes of reality. There is the physical world (body), the psychic (emotions) and spiritual (noetic); within each of these planes, additionally, we have the interaction of universal mind and our own consciousness.

Additionally, according to mystics, we are more complex and have an etheric body double in each of these three planes. This etheric body is comprised of ether or the energy of creation. This etheric energy gives life, in the earth phase, to our present body, soul, emotions and consciousness.

When we speak about the completed man or woman, we speak about the person who is master of the three spheres or planes of existence. This person has united their etheric self with their worldly self, on all three planes. When the mystic speaks about uniting with their higher soul, they speak of unity with their noetic self. This part is always in tune with Truth, but because of the noise or discordance of the lower selves, it cannot hear itself speak.

We have to still the noise of everyday life so we can hear the timeless aspect within ourselves. That is the inner journey and when it is completed the mystic returns that much more able to serve. The wise ones say wisdom is of no use unless it is put to work in the world.

## 67. What is consciousness?

Many define consciousness as logical and sequential thought. However in our discussion consciousness has a wider aspect. Consciousness is energy that is self-aware; in man / woman, this consciousness is aware of itself on three planes / levels. For most people this awareness is confined primarily to awareness in / of the earth phase. Spiritually the learning that is required is expansion into our own existence in the etheric spheres. We learn about this through our etheric double, expansion of consciousness and knowledge of Truth. For when we learn about the higher aspects of self, we learn about Truth. Part of us is a small piece of the Absolute or universal mind. This part has eternal existence.

Ordinarily our worldly consciousness is limited and has only partial self-awareness. Examples of this include: awareness of *bodily functions* like breathing and heart beat (some of which is on a subconscious level), pain, pleasure, five senses, sexual experience and exercise; awareness of our *emotions* such as joy, anger and happiness; awareness through *thought processes* such as comparison, logic, problem solving and sequential thought; and *spiritual awareness,* example of this experience are states / feelings of oneness and higher aspects of meditative practice.

Also consciousness is multi-dimensional and occurs simultaneously in combinations of levels / planes. For example, when we are in love, we feel it emotionally, physically and spiritually. Also when we are problem solving and logically come to a long sought conclusion, we feel relieved and happy.

Daily experience, through conscious awareness, is felt simultaneously on various levels of our physical existence and as we journey, we expand our consciousness into the etheric planes.

# 68. This sort of learning seems totally beyond me. Can you make this simpler?

In all learning there are degrees to which one knows something. The more you learn, the simpler knowledge about self becomes.

In our discussion, if something does not call to you or seems unnecessary or too complicated let it be. Take from this discussion what is useful, what you can apply to your life just to get you started.

In time, if your learning path requires that you learn something more, you will be able to pick the fruit.

In this journey, all that is essential is already inside of you. You have been given enough for the journey. Turn inward and listen to the quiet whisper. Along with grace and mercy from Truth, this is all you need.

## 69. In some traditions, people withdraw from the world to increase spiritual learning. Some join a monastery. Should I do this?

We cannot all go off to join the monastery. Who would take care of the little ones and feed them? Who would cut the grass or deliver the pizzas? Some of us are called to retreat from the world, but many of us are not.

Today, some Orders are allowing their followers to have jobs in the everyday world. This allows for individual expression.

Each has an individual path and one is not better than another. Enlightenment can be found anywhere in the world; the world is a giant classroom and one finds God changing a diaper and another, repeating litanies to the Holy One.

For most, withdrawal from the world is an inner experience and occurs during quiet, reflective time. The physical withdrawal or going away to monastery is an outward manifestation of this inward connection.

There are others who go through their daily affairs and have kept a part of them selves connected, One with God. These people have learned to participate in the world and make each action a prayer; part of themselves is always praying and in tune with Truth. This withdrawal is an inner connection into unity with God; hence their action, or work in this world, is aligned.

# 70. What advice can you give for spiritual parents looking to raise spiritually aware children?

The advice that I offer for raising your children, is essentially the same advice I offer to you.

- Teach your children how to travel to the different parts of themselves and how to listen to their own inner song. Teach them to be excellent at something.
- Embrace one of the great faiths so you can one day travel beyond surface / primary teachings. The journey is that of learning about self and expanding into higher consciousness. Within each of the great faiths there is an inner teaching.
- If the child cannot embrace one of the great traditions, teach them to be a good human being and search for their spiritual teacher. Purity and sincerity of heart, engenders spiritual learning.
- Each soul enters the earth phase to learn, work, love and serve. Teach your children about their destiny, then, let them live it.
- Teach your children about social and individual responsibility. As a human being we have basic responsibilities to self and others.
- Encourage your children to experience the many parts of them self and that reality is far greater than what they see before them.
- Show your children how to pray and transcend fear. Teach them how to make their life the prayer.
- Teach your children they are eternal and are sons / daughters of a King. Their destiny is to govern

the vast kingdom of self and return to the King more complete.
- The earth phase is to experience and learn. Show your children how to make their lives an exciting hour of joy and celebration. The inner journey begins by remembering who we are.
- Teach your children they cannot die. The physical death is but a door into another existence of self.

# 71. How does a soul come to know its destiny?

Each soul has a destiny that is both collective and individual. We live within a social group and must contribute to its upkeep as well as developing inner potential.

We learn about responsibility to community through family, friends, school, church and town / city. Also we learn through presentations in the media about life around us.

Within each soul is knowledge of its individual destiny. Some are born with this in their waking consciousness; if you ask them, they wish to be a famous singer, a doctor or a mother. Others are less sure and their destiny is more of a mystery. Each is born with individual talents and predisposition toward life direction and experience. Each soul enters with a life plan to both gain experience and contribute.

The environment can influence and even alter these preset directions. That is why educators and child psychologists advocate a loving and supportive home environment.

Spiritually for each soul to mature and grow in development of self there must be quiet time for self reflection. Also there has to be teaching and a structure that supports this learning. That is why formal religion is so important, even if later the child rejects part or all of it. The groundwork and basic principles are offered and it is a place to begin.

In the journey to completion, all cultures teach ideas or beliefs that must be temporarily shed. These ideas or cultural imperatives are part of the structure and indoctrination system that is required to maintain our culture. In this culture one of the operant philosophies or myths, is that, in order to be successful you need a good job, be happily married, with a house in the suburbs and two children. This myth incorporates many of the values that are essential to our sociological and capitalistic way of life. These are intended as vehicles to keep the culture operant and are extended too far when they are presented as the only choices. There is so much more than this, on a spiritual level, to achieve in life.

Spiritually, many cultural imperatives need to be shed, or placed aside, for a time. This is different than discarding them for good. The reason for this is that attached to cultural imperatives, value systems, or religious training is strong emotions that block inner perception. Higher consciousness will not operate when strong ideas or emotions are present. The call of the higher self is often a soft, gentle pull.

It is the teacher that helps the student navigate and walk this minefield. Certain ideas hold us back, certain ideas are helpful. The teacher knows not only what conventions are not helpful but when and under what circumstances they should be discarded and replaced with newer insights.

That is why all traditions urge the necessity of a teacher and quiet time for reflection, prayer and meditation.

Before beginning quiet time, the student is told to bathe or change into clean clothing. This symbolizes a cleansing of worldly self (dirt from work, ideas and emotions) so that which is fainter or more fragile might be perceived. The prayer or meditative device is a focus point to fix the worldly consciousness; still the daily pattern of thought and let that which is waiting come forward.

Remember, we are the door that blocks our way and, in part, structure exists so it might be transcended.

## 72. Rare is the day when I am not fearful or anxious about something. When this happens, I grow tense; all of this is very uncomfortable. How is fear helpful and what spiritual purpose does it serve?

Fear is part of our biological and emotional hardware. Over millions of years, our reaction to danger, called the fight or flight response, has developed to help keep us alive; in our environment, we are acutely sensitive to any threat, no matter how small. In part, that is why we have survived over millions of years.

The fight or flight response triggers a number of

physical and emotional reactions. Against the perceived danger, instantly we evaluate our chance of success, and either prepare to make a stand and fight or run away. Typically when we see danger, our adrenaline begins to flow, our heart beats faster and we grow acutely attentive; emotional and physical systems go on alert status and we decide instantly what to do.

When fear is felt for a period of time, it develops into anxiety or malaise. Sometimes this anxiety is general we do not consciously know the cause. Sometimes anxiety is very specific. However nervousness is intended to be a protective and 'get us ready' device; that is why we are uncomfortable. Part of us is saying, you are on alert status; there is a perceived danger and decide whether to fight or flight. In some professions this nervousness is so common there is a name for it. Actors call it 'opening night jitters' and acknowledge this anxiety helps them concentrate on their lines.

When we are not consciously aware of the source, anxiety and fear can be problematic. Prolonged anxiety, unless properly channeled, can lead to a number of emotional complications and illness.

Spiritually it is important to understand the source of fear because like other powerful thoughts and emotions, they block the higher consciousness. When one is comfortable with their spiritual path, there is no fear or anxiety, only peace, Light and higher knowledge.

## 73. Why do things change and seemingly remain in motion?

Change is dynamic, and motion speaks to an aspect of the Divine. Our body and spirit, each are a small world that is forever moving and evolving. Cells are replaced, blood flows through our veins, food is eaten, digested, turned into energy and expelled as waste. Our thoughts and desires shift like the weather; one moment we like this person, the next we are angry, then we make-up and are in love again.

The point of the cycle of birth and death is evolution; over time, we are changing into a more advanced spirit. Also each day we are reborn into a new life and have the opportunity to be any number of things. In this development, like the caterpillar that becomes a butterfly, we evolve into a beautiful creature that soars across the meadow.

## 74. Why is it important to give to others? Some religions request a percent of your wage as regular donation.

The universe as we know it could not exist without giving. Giving is natural and is another aspect of the Divine. Just as a mother gives life to her child, freely offers milk and guidance through the years, so, we must learn to give of ourselves. In giving to others, without expectation, we are living our higher destiny.

On the spiritual level, when the higher comes forward, we are in tune with Truth. This occurs so we can be of service and give whatever is needed. For an example, look at the lives of the Servants of God. Each had a vocation and their life involved helping others reach higher. Some helped with sickness, others with guidance, or providing spiritual Light to those who were in darkness.

Give freely to others, without expectation or indebtedness and you will discover who you are. True 'service' is a medicine against our feelings of self importance. Humility is a key that unlocks spiritual doors.

# 75. Why do people disagree and start wars over religious beliefs? How can both sides be right?

First let us keep in mind that people start wars over all kinds of things; usually the reasons for a war are both complex and simple; these involving economic resources, philosophical / religious differences and behavioral factors (pride, revenge). Also the actual reasons for a war are usually hidden from the people who have to fight the war and the most popular or politically useful justification is made public. We see this daily in the news. But we can also see it on a smaller level in the interactions we have with people in our daily lives.

Now can two things be right or correct at the same time? Yes. On lower levels of reality this is possible and we see it all the time. Consider the married couple who wants to go on vacation. One person wants to go to Europe and the other wishes to visit friends who live near Disneyworld in Florida. Both are entitled to their opinion and in this matter are right; yet in order to go on vacation together some type of compromise is required.

Obviously, on higher levels of reality, Truth is singular; however in the earth phase Truth manifests in multiple ways so it might be known.

Yet some religions assert their way is correct and others are wrong and non-believers risk going to hell. This is different than deciding where to go on a family vacation. Here we find the same scenario. The religious leader, who asserts this is the only way, interprets the reality as he perceives it. At his / her level this is his / her view, however, no prophet came and brought a teaching framed in this manner; this claim is another's interpretation of an original teaching. All prophets come to bring the *current path* to the Absolute; this way or path has both an external and internal reality. The external reality is bound to time and place, while the internal is unifying and transcendent. Hence, in paths, we observe differences and similarities. This is how both sides can be "right."

When viewing monotheism and the message of prophets, it is important to remember, Jesus came to rekindle the 'old tradition' because it required renewal; he did not come to start a new religion. Mohammed came to present the aspect of surrender to the desert people who had strayed far from decency; at the time, this required a self-defensive and war effort as many resisted this teaching and wished to kill Mohammed. In fact, Islam is known as the religion of surrender to God; the Koran mentions both Christians and Jews who are strong in this quality and they are to be left alone free to worship.

In our scenario about going on vacation, for the vacation to work, there must be a compromise of sorts; this might involve going to both places, or taking turns in subsequent yearly trips.

In the world of political / religious philosophy we are dealing with fanatics and self-serving governments. Sadly many have not reached the awareness that we must accept a fair compromise; and each person is entitled to worship as long as they do not harm or limit others.

# 76. If I am dissatisfied with my path, how do I find another?

In this matter, there are a number of considerations. Because you are dissatisfied with something it does not mean it is not of use; dissatisfaction is an emotional state which can come and go. Ask yourself what you dislike about your religious presentation; usually, the part we dislike is a specific person or particular aspect of the teaching; this is usually a surface dimension, or interpretation that has angered and hurt us.

Yet, spiritual experience is independent of teachers or teachings. Spiritual learning and experience is an inner acknowledgement of our own higher capacity. It is an inner perception and awareness that is buried within and independent of clergy, teachers, or teachings.

Remember, to reach higher knowledge we need a structure to learn; each has to be careful not to go running between learning environments, never finding the right setting, because they were the wrong kind of student: a student who never finds the right teaching because the different teachings did not fit his preconceived notions and standards. This is not the purpose of learning!

A teaching may be measured, that is, a determination made if it is the correct teaching for you in a number of ways. Just like buying a car, each of us has very specific external requirements. We must be consciously aware of these requirements, list them, and try not to let them operate subconsciously.

For example, some people learn best when their teacher is a man rather than a woman. Others are more open to learning when the format incorporates their existing faith and others when it is from another culture and 'exotic.'

Internally, you will be aware if the path is working for you; there will be an inner spiritual acknowledgement, because this experience and learning is part of the design of your life.

If this is not present and there is an internal discord, stop your searching and turn inward. It is not the time for you. Sincerely ask your higher self for guidance and as your life unfolds, your path will find you.

It is a spiritual rule that the teacher calls to the student and finds them. The part that the teacher perceives and activates must be aligned with the spiritual impulse. This spiritual alignment is achieved through honest seeking, right living and internal preparation.

As in daily life, on a spiritual level, you must earn what you receive.

## 77. Each of the great faiths has a holy book. What can you say about them?

The books are intended to be a joy and source of inspiration, bringing comfort to the reader. Often they are recorded by followers of a great tradition or written by the teacher. Each is filled with light, energy and healing. Traditionally presented through a revelation from a spiritual source; these great works provide a basis for daily life, are incomparable and affect us on many levels.

When reading these wonderful books, note the following cautions. These teachings emanate from God, but to enter our world, the world of forms, require filtering through at least two others; one to voice the revelation and another to record it. In this filtering process, often aspects alter; remember spirit changes to enter the world of forms.

Second many of these writings have been translated from one language to another. Often in translating, meanings of specific words shift and are left out or not completely understood. Much of this is unintentional, but the reader must be cautious, before accepting every word as holy dictum.

Third, passages, sections and entire books have been left out of certain translations. Some of this is intentional to influence people in specific directions.

Fourth, specific teachings and revelations, while transcendent and universal, are given to a specific people at a given time and place. Some of the social problems these teachings target are not prevalent in all societies, at other times, and these marvelous books have to be understood in this context.

For example, at the time of Mohammed, the desert people worshipped multiple gods and practiced female infanticide; specific sections of the glorious Koran admonish against these destructive behaviors. While other sections of the Koran, particularly the sections on submission, easily transition to our society, other sections do not. Also another problematic factor is a government that is based upon religious teaching; in many countries, including our own, there is a separation of 'church and state.'

Let me offer a suggestion to the spiritual traveler. Read all of the books by each of the great faiths. Try to get your hands on the best translation available to you. These are usually available at a large local library. Number the points on which the great faiths agree and number the points on which they disagree.

If this is too daunting a task, then initially focus your energy on the Old Testament, the New Testament and then the Koran. Start somewhere!

Keep in mind the limitations of time and place, possible errors of translation, and work under the assumption that it is possible that all these faiths work and help believers reach Truth. And after you have done your tallying of differences and similarities, ask yourself this last question.

Today in the world, who is causing the discord between people of different faiths and for what reason?

After you have done your own research all of this will become clearer.

# 78. How is it possible for each of the great faiths to work? I am still having trouble with this.

It is a matter of belief; if you take as true or work for something hard enough and the energy is aligned with universal potential- it happens. By making the statement, the great faiths work we mean that prayers are granted and these faiths help people draw closer to the Absolute.

Researchers have begun to examine the relationship between prayer, belief and spontaneous healing. They are questioning people who have been 'miraculously' healed after going to a holy man / woman or famous shrine; the researchers are trying to identify the factors that are operating. Their hypothesis is focused on belief and what happens, phenomenally, when we *strongly* believe something; testing energy patterns, brain waves and questioning eyewitnesses.

Over the last few years, a number of research studies have been conducted concerning the phenomena of distant healing; similarly the researchers are trying to isolate the operating factors and a number of studies, have demonstrated the power of prayer, scientifically. Some of these studies have been double blind designs and volunteers from all religious faiths have been used as healers. So each great faith has been proven to work! We live in age where science has begun to validate the efficacy of belief, prayer and religion.

From a mystical perspective, when we believe or take as true something strongly enough, or intensely visualize it to its smallest detail, intense energy is created. This energy seeks a conduit and if this desire /

belief / prayer finds the right conduit in the universal possibility, it comes true / materializes in the earth phase.

There is a story that is told about an honest, sincere man who went to request intervention at a local saint's shrine. He prayed for restored health of a family member and, because it was an unselfish prayer, his request was granted.

A famous teacher when questioned about this phenomenon and what laws were operating responded in this way. "All around this tomb, in energy and thought forms, were the collected prayers of hundreds of supplicants. Waiting for the prayer energy of a sincere person, the other energy joined along with the potential of the situation. Thus his prayer was answered and a 'miraculous' cure took place. These are natural laws that few today understand or are able to use."

We must keep in mind that each of the great faiths is a conduit to the Absolute. This is their function.

# 79. Are you saying that prayers being answered are simply the operation of natural laws? If they are so natural, why don't we all just know them?

Yes. Remember the mystics call the conscious, purposeful spiritual development of humanity, 'the science of man / woman.' How prayer operates is one example of this science. According to the mystics, once spiritual laws are understood there is nothing miraculous or extraordinary about their workings.

This higher knowledge is closely guarded and cannot be made available to anyone unless they earn and are prepared for it. Part of the preparation is sincerity of effort; this sincerity cannot be manufactured or faked. In this way the higher knowledge protects itself from those who would misuse it.

Once you have learned that which you came here to learn: that is the first step. Next you must put this knowledge to work.

The wise are those who serve out of love; making their lives an extension of the Divine Will. These natural laws work in conjunction with the actions of those serving the Divine Will.

# 80. Some people are fond of quoting God as a justification for advocating certain action or beliefs. They urge God says this or God says that. Can you comment upon this?

In my work in the psychiatric hospitals I have met people who claim to have spoken with God. Unfortunately because of their obvious distress and present circumstance, it is difficult to take their accounts seriously.

In the history of the great faiths, prophets have communicated directly with God and their experience is recorded in the great books. For example, Moses had an encounter with God, as did Mohammed both of these events are detailed. Any message God has for humanity is offered in similar accounts.

Outside of a prophet's experience with God, it is rare that a saint has a similar encounter. Usually messages are sent through intermediaries in the form of inspiration or revelation.

These messages, while emanating from God, are not the 'word of God;' texts of a first-hand encounter.

Many faiths have traditions that are sayings attributed to God. An example of one: "God says, if you take one step toward me I will take ten toward you." This saying highlights God's mercy and is intended to remind believers of God's love. These are traditional sayings and convey a particular aspect of God's nature. They may not be direct quotes, in a factual sense.

In our earlier discussion concerning the great books, we discussed some of the problems that exist when considering entire texts as the literal word of God. Here with the sayings of God, we present the same limitations. Keep in mind that if someone is quoting God, many times, their motivation for doing so is more important that what they are actually saying.

# 81. I have heard different versions of what the afterlife will be like. How can all of these versions be true? Which account is factual?

Again we have to be careful not to impose our own limitations or the traditional interpretation of the teachings of our faith, on the situation. Perhaps all the accounts are true and the afterlife is a variety of experiences. Or as the mystic asserts, a reality we create ourselves.

Consciousness is energy and energy has a life of its own. One of the present laws of physics asserts that energy is neither destroyed nor created; in our universe, therefore, energy has a permanent existence.

When I close my eyes and concentrate real hard imagining myself on a tropical island, I am creating a thought form, called an elemental, which has existence. In my mind, for a brief time, I am on this island and, after I have gone on to another thought, this island vacation thought form exists in the world until it returns to me or I actually go on this vacation.

Traditional teaching asserts that the afterlife contains seven heavens and within these heavens there are many layers.

Remember our fundamental nature is conscious energy, which at its core is aligned with God. In fact most traditions assert this heart or core is a small piece of the Godhead. In our minds (consciousness), daily, we create all sorts of worlds and when we pass over we take with us the worlds we have created.

Because some of the clergy have used fear to control people, they paint the picture of an afterlife that is limiting. They warn, 'if you do not follow our teachings you will go to hell and if you do follow our teaching, you will live forever in heaven.'

I cannot tell you what to believe. Neither can I describe the afterlife. What I offer is the possibility that what you have been taught might not be the entire picture; there are alternate teachings. You need to make your own decision about this matter after researching and learning on your own or with a teacher.

## 82. Recently our science has proven that each atom, for the most part, is comprised of empty space. Consequently what we perceive as solid is not completely solid at all. So if I am sitting in a chair, am I really sitting in a chair, or the idea of a chair?

According to the mystic, much of what we have been taught about the nature of reality is not accurate. It is a partial account that has been slanted to guide and control us in socially accepted directions. If you think about it, you can probably conclude that this is useful in some ways and harmful in others.

While what we do and accomplish in the earth phase is extremely important and impacts upon the next, this is only part of the reality.

The earth phase, or physical reality, is comprised of conscious energy that vibrates at a level low enough to where it becomes dense and forms into matter. This matter has different sub-frequencies. Overall, this vibration level, compared to other more spiritual worlds, is at a relatively low frequency. The higher worlds vibrate at a higher (faster) frequency and one can enter these worlds, while still in the body, by raising the speed of the vibration level.

In order to enter the earth phase our soul took on a physical body; this body vibrates at the level of physical matter and consequently we are able to interact in this world and to answer the question, "Am I sitting in a chair?"

Let me offer an often used example to help explain part of this concept. All around us there are radio waves. These waves are invisible and we do not notice or feel them because their vibration is such that we are physically unaware of their existence. However, once we turn on our radio, which is attuned to a certain frequency (vibration) we have music. The radio is able to bring into our room, if you will, something of another dimension, which up to this point we were not consciously aware of. These waves were as real as our body but because we had not activated the tuning mechanism, we could not perceive them.

This is what the mystic asserts about reality. All around there are worlds that we are not consciously interacting with; however they are more real or lasting, than the world of forms. It is a matter of tuning our consciousness; because of self-serving powerful institutions, this reality has been left out of our education.

Let us suppose for a moment, everything we see about us is an illusion and the things we come in contact with will no longer be there when we awake on the morning.

What will we do? Will we laugh or cry? Will we be happy for this experience or will we want more? Will we have sweet or bitter memories? How will these experiences prepare us for our real lives?

Give thought to this proposition; it is not very far from the Truth.

## 83. How will the spiritual teaching vary based upon people's needs? Will I find teaching that speaks to me directly?

Remember in this journey you are not responsible for how another understands the eternal mysteries and moves toward God. This is the responsibility of each soul and everyone is exactly at the level they should be. Understanding of the Absolute is both inborn and learned through effort.

There are many others, in many worlds, whose responsibility is the monitoring of souls and depending upon individual effort, deeper understanding is afforded them.

Why do you think there are so many beliefs and teachers? People are different, learn at individual rates, and vary in desire to understand and reconcile mysteries. Depending on the level of your desire and ability to learn, your teacher will guide the teaching so that it resonates with your soul.

## 84. How is each soul unique and how does each soul become aware of its place in the universe?

Each of us is a unique expression of Truth. There is none like us, nor will there ever be another exactly like us. We develop, at our own pace, in understanding of our cosmic potential. While we are similar in many ways, we are a singular combination of wants, desires, talents and universal consciousness that has developed over millennia.

There is an old saying 'you cannot step into the same river twice.' While on the surface, the water appears the same, below there is an interplay of factors that is forever changing. Due to the currents, the stream's bottom is shifting. Fish are swimming, plants are growing and temperature is rising and falling. The water itself is filled with different nutrients that relate to the composition of soil upriver and across the countryside multiple elements have been added or dumped into the river.

As discussed earlier, this unfolding of knowledge is on many levels. Each is born with an inner, spiritual understanding of their relationship to Truth and what they must accomplish. This awareness of the cosmic potential is brought to what we call consciousness, gradually and at different rates for each learner. This rate of learning is dependent upon the traveler's effort and their role in the cosmic design.

Each traveler is a unique being and as such has an individual learning sequence. All travelers are on the path to completion. This is the Divine Command and the mission for which each soul was created and sent out into the universe. Each soul is to travel and return more complete so they can reign in Kingship. The universe governed is oneself and when one has become master of self- other responsibilities are added.

## 85. What role does religion play in keeping people healthy and free from illness?

Each of the great traditions, in part, defines what is necessary for a balanced life; some religions are very specific about what actions to avoid. Traditional teachings vary and include social, personal and moral prescriptions for the larger society. The intent is to order the society and provide a framework around which the individual can build a healthy spiritual life.

Different religious traditions emphasize these prescriptions in varying amounts which were intended for a specific audience and time; some of these prescriptions have become traditional and have made their way into modern culture.

An example of this was the injunction to eat meat that had been slaughtered only in a specific manner and within three days of the animal's death. This tradition requires that prayers are said over the animal and a member of the clergy supervises its preparation. The original reason for this tradition grew out of health factors; this was before the age of refrigeration and many became sick eating meat that had decayed. Animals developed unhealthy bacteria and this prescription was offered before the aspect of bacteriologic decay was fully understood; many believed the meat was sanctified by their clergy and, eating only specific animals and fish, brought them closer to their God and prevented illness.

This tradition has survived into present day. Today we no longer have the problem of decayed meat; however people follow this prescription because they believe it brings them closer to their God.

Another prescription for healthy living centered on the activity of giving. In weekly collections, the individual was urged to make a percent of their wage available to the church and larger community. This was intended to teach the individual about selfless giving and help further the church's work. This is another tradition that has made its way into modern day.

Recent research with volunteers suggests that selfless giving engenders good feelings, which many suspect lead toward the prevention of illness. There is something in the alchemy of giving (without resentment) that boosts immune function.

Another prescription by most faiths has been the advice to live moderately and not to overdo sensual pleasure. We live in an age, where many have been affected by negative consequences of not following this advice. Our society has multiple problems with eating disorders, use of illegal drugs, alcoholism and sexual addiction.

Many faiths urge that individuals marry, build and adhere to strong familial bonds. Today we know that in order for a person to lead a rich emotional life, they need to be around people that will nourish them and help prevent extended loneliness. One of the joys of a rich familial life is loving people who are there for you in difficult times. This type of social support is necessary for everyone and is one of the factors that help prevent emotional stress and physical illness.

Over the last decades, research has emerged that has highlighted the positive healthy effect of transcendental meditation (TM), certain forms of physical yoga and prayer. Early work on TM brought into focus how this simple 'religious' exercise could boost immune function, reduce stress and help prevent all sorts of illnesses. Additionally when TM was incorporated with the individual's belief system (prayer), these effects were even more dramatic. For millennia, religious leaders have been exhorting people to pray regularly; in our age we are just beginning to understand the different dimensions to this traditional activity.

According to the mystical tradition, illness originates in the soul and manifests physically and emotionally in the body as well. Spiritual reasons for illness are many; some of which include repaying karmic debt, a learning that is required, an obstacle that needs to be overcome, depletion of etheric energy due to worry or the eventual cause of death.

Our science has made tremendous strides in understanding the physical and emotional dimensions to illness. Holistic approaches to medicine require that modern healers understand and incorporate this spiritual dimension. This combination of factors, the interplay of the three spheres, will lead to a new frontier in understanding medicine and who we really are.

## 86. Can you elaborate on free will and how this relates to the concept of a life by design?

As discussed, what distinguishes man from other creations is the capacity to make our own decisions. Each person can choose their destiny, within specific parameters, if they wish to serve God.

In establishing a life-plan, before birth, we decide what areas we would like to further develop, i.e., learn about how this will assist us in our journey back to God. In order to accomplish the learning that is required, we bring along with us certain skills and abilities. All of this is freely chosen and if we choose not to reincarnate, at this time, usually we are free not to do this as well.

Now, when we get to this plane of existence, we make our decisions based upon our life plan, the skills we brought with us and the designs that are emerging. According to certain traditions, the number of designs, or patterns available, is fixed and everything that occurs in the earth phase is a variation of basic patterns.

To further illustrate, let us present an example of a young man who has entered the earth phase, to learn in part about self-sacrifice. His life plan calls for him to get married and have four children. This will require saving money and using most of his time away from work helping guide the members of his family. The skills he has brought along with him, to achieve this learning goal, are an innate sense of salesmanship and likeability.

However, as he approaches the age to enter a career and eventually marry, the country that he has chosen to live in has entered a period of recession. Positions as a salesman are difficult to find; the few that are opening are in the computer industry and our young man has never been very good at math or understanding computers.

Yet, in order to follow his life-plan, he subconsciously knows he must take the position and enter the computer field, which had economic times been better, he would have avoided. In order to become successful, he enrolls in Business College to increase his knowledge about computers; in time, with hard work and perseverance, he becomes one of the company's top salesmen.

In the process of enrolling in Business College, he meets his future wife, and learns about perseverance, sticking to something that is difficult to accomplish, another of his life's learning goals.

All along, this fellow was free to make his own decisions. These decisions were influenced by the emerging economic design (a period of recession), and his own, inner sense (life-plan) of what he wanted to accomplish. This fellow could have chosen not to accept the position as a computer salesman, but because of hard times, he realized he was lucky to have this opportunity. Accordingly, he voluntarily raised his skills in understanding computers and entering Business College; while he worked, this activity helped him move toward reaching other life goals.

The outcome of our lives is not preset; it is a potential that we set ourselves and work toward. However, we cannot wake-up one day and decide to be a brain surgeon, unless this was a latent potential (part of our life-plan). There are requirements of the situation. Do we have the scientific and educational background necessary for medical school? Are the financial resources in place for us to carry this off? Will we be any good at the work?

Yes we are free to choose, but only within the framework of the situation. Also, we do not know the outcome, unless we try. Your Life Plan does not require that you do something dramatic. It requires that you do something purposeful and become someone who is useful. The servant seeks to serve and be of use.

## 87. Is a spiritually completed person, one who has achieved God Consciousness, a God? This is what some traditions claim.

First, we must identify limitations in our discussion. The claims of different traditions have to be viewed from within that tradition. It is very difficult for an observer to understand or fully comprehend what is operating unless the observer has first-hand experience; we operate under the assumption that all faiths are true at a certain level.

Also, it is very difficult to put into words a spiritual state, or a spiritual level that one has not yet attained. However, useful comparisons may be made. Last, we must take into account historical perspective. When each of the great faiths was initiated and when the title of 'god' was conferred, the term may have meant something a little different than what it means today in our monotheistic culture. Many cultures acknowledge the existence of spiritual entities that govern plants, forests and mountains. In these traditions, there are different levels of 'gods' and 'gods' for all natural phenomena.

With our strides in science and present focus upon exploration of self and religion, we are beginning to understand some of these miraculous 'phenomena' as an extension of natural laws. Interestingly enough, that is what the wise ones have always said concerning their 'miracles.'

The outcome of all mystery traditions and human development systems is the completed person. In some traditions, these spiritually developed individuals are called Buddha, Sadhu, enlightened one, servant of God, saint, mystic or heretic. Yet, what each of these people has in common is they have achieved a level of spiritual development, which in the context of their faith, is extraordinary. Along with this level of spiritual development are capacities that appear miraculous, simply because they are not understood. Yet, the person who uses these capacities, when questioned, describes them as extensions of natural laws, which they intuitively and purposefully direct to carry out their function.

Also, part of the confusion surrounding this issue comes about due to specific statements made by individuals who were deemed highly spiritually developed. Some of these statements were termed heretical and people were executed for making them.

Part of the mystical path is a state called annihilation. In this state, the worldly consciousness is annihilated or destroyed and the spirit is unified and briefly becomes one with Truth / God. In this state, if the person should speak, sometimes the energy is so strong and joyous, they assert out loud, "I Am The Way," or, "I Am The Truth."

When this happens, it is not the person speaking, but the spirit or energy that is moving through them, asserting itself. This energy is the Logos, or Spirit of God; for this energy, or Light, is the binding force of the universe and is the Way and the Truth. It is suggested that Jesus, in part, was killed for making this statement. Similarly, a Muslim Saint, Al-Hallaj was disemboweled for making this claim.

From our perspective, that which is greater than the universe is different than that which is created. Although a part of God is in everyone, no matter how well advanced a spiritual entity; we are not the Creator or the same as the Creator.

Some traditions assert the Logos takes on a human form to carry out its mission. Perhaps, this is true and this is a wonderful event, however, is this, the same as the Creator entering the world of forms? Each must come to a decision about this on their own, and, it is suggested, the event be viewed within the context of the specific faith asserting this.

## 88. No matter what you assert, how can this be the way the world is supposed to be; it's a real mess out there. How will the mystical view help our modern world? Is there a place for mysticism in times like these?

According to mystical tradition, this view is the balancing factor. It is the missing ingredient and the pot of gold at rainbow's end. This viewpoint balances the needs of the individual with the need of the larger society; it reconciles the differences in religious philosophies. The experience of the Light is unifying and life changing.

If you perceive the world as being in a state of confusion, remember the following: what you see before you is a stage in evolution; we are evolving into something higher. Each has a contribution to make; that is part of the journey. What will be your contribution? Remember each contribution is necessary for the completed work.

If you do not believe these claims, test them for yourself and begin your learning. You will see, in time, the world will become a better place.

# 89. What does the term enlightenment mean? Is this the goal of the mystical process?

As previously discussed, the goal of the mystical process is the spiritually complete person who is better able to serve in the world.

By products of this developmental process are abilities and capacities that people term supra normal. These are necessary for the mystic to perform his or her function and vary within each person.

The term enlightenment relates to the mystic's spiritual condition, where he / she has been infused with Light and knowledge to dissipate their own darkness. In some traditions, this infusion of Light and knowledge occurs in a glorious burst and in other traditions, the process is more gradual. Light and knowledge are infused, slowly, until the mystic is internally aglow and, externally, becomes a beacon for the dark night.

In order for the mystic to become enlightened, a number of factors must be in place. Some of these have already been discussed; however, it is generally acknowledged there are internal roadblocks that the mystic must temporarily remove, so his / her own Inner Light can manifest. Some of these roadblocks are superficial desires, thoughts and misconceptions concerning the process.

Each society, in order for it to operate effectively, advances myths and defines operating rules to reach mutually agreed goals. These rules and goals, over time, combine into a generally accepted social contract and the workings of this contract, in a society, can govern the way a person leads their life.

For example, one country agrees, it is a capitalistic society and consequently strives for free enterprise where individual acquisition of wealth is prized. Another country is founded upon a set of principles that are more socialistic; where it is the responsibility of government to assure a more balanced distribution of wealth. To this end, the government owns industry and health services, assuring that everybody receives a basic minimum standard.

In our discussion, what is important, are the thoughts, feelings, and emotional investment around these social contracts and societal myths. For it is precisely this emotional attachment around the fixed belief system that must be pushed aside, for a brief time, so the mystic can reach his goal. Further these ideas need to be understood, so they can be disarmed and brushed aside so something else can come forward.

It is like there is a door between the mystic and the prize (higher knowledge). This door is deep inside and must be pushed aside (opened) so something else can come forward. In part, the door is made up of our belief system and our attachments (emotional investment) to these beliefs. The door cannot be thrown away or destroyed; it is necessary in our society for daily life. Consequently a more subtle approach is necessary; this is what the mystic learns, under the supervision of the teacher.

In our present society a number of myths and social contracts center on materialism (economic wealth), sexuality and self-fulfillment. As an example, and previously discussed, this is how one of our myths and social contracts was stated: *Perhaps, if I work real hard, get a good job (make money), get married (find romantic love), have a house and two children, then, I will be happy (self-fulfillment)?*

From the mystical perspective, there is nothing wrong with this ideal; all societies have their version and these types of ideals are necessary to keep things moving along. What is important is that the person understands how these powerful beliefs are operating on the consciousness and can they push aside the effects, temporarily, so something else can emerge.

It is possible to reach enlightenment in everyday life, but only when certain conditions are met. Many of these conditions, center on consciousness and removal of what is blocking the inner capacity from coming forward.

# 90. In my inner development, how do I know if I am advancing? What criteria can be used to measure progress?

Everyone is moving forward and evolving. That is the nature of the universe. If a path has not opened to you, pray and follow the teachings of your religion. If you are not able to do this, then be a good person and devote some time to going inward and helping others. Then, as events unfold, a door will open. Higher knowledge is our destiny and is as natural as breathing.

If you are on a path or following the teachings of your religion and want criteria against which to measure your actions, feel free to use the following. If an action, or thought, brings you closer to God / Truth than follow / accept it. If it distances you, let it be.

A second criterion concerns how you feel and what you think about most often. If you feel happier and think of God / Truth frequently, you are probably advancing. Keep in mind, however, it is possible to think about something too much and become fixated; we are striving for a balanced life.

# 91. What is the outcome of a life? And how does this relate to Judgment Day?

Much of the answer to the first question has been dealt with. The outcome of a life is movement either toward or away from one's higher potential and the higher destiny of the universe. From a mystical perspective, simply stated, the outcome is movement toward the Absolute and service to others. That is the criterion.

As the soul goes over its life and prepares for the next stage, an evaluation and decision making process is undertaken. This review has no time limit or fixed result. We all have free will and must evaluate and decide the outcome of our actions. Did we live in accord with a higher call or did we distance ourselves, giving in to our lower nature? We all have inner tools to make this assessment and will be given guidance as required. In the next stage, everyone has further work in reaching his or her own higher potential.

Will there be a collective Judgment Day? This is a question that you must answer for yourself. It is possible multiple evaluations and choices will occur.

O the pain of death and the moment of bitterness as the soul leaves the body. What parent wants this for their child?

Yet we are not thinking in the right way. This life is a prison for the soul and the moment of release is a joyous one. The soul is returning home. Learn to think of this moment as a release into a greater freedom. Forget the worldly consciousness, and focus on the transcendent. Even as it relates to your children; especially as it relates to your children.

You ask why it must be so. I tell you your mind cannot understand. You must experience the answer with your heart; this is all part of the Universal Plan.

# 92. What is the relationship between giving and healthy selfishness?

Exploration and development of self is the primary focus of the mystical process. We are learning about ourselves so we can learn about and serve the Absolute.

In recent years, a psychological concept, called healthy selfishness has been identified and underscores knowing what we need to make ourselves happy and engaging in those behaviors is an important aspect to healthy living.

For some people, giving to others is an important link in their personal happiness and health. Volunteers who weekly give to others report improved feelings of self-esteem and happiness; they report helping others makes them feel good and these good feelings, in a number of research studies, have been identified as immune boosters. Volunteers, in these studies, suffer with fewer illnesses and go to the doctor less frequently. A key element in this sort of giving is that there is no expectation attached. It is freely bestowed, without indebtedness.

So it seems, for some people, that giving unselfishly to others might be in our own best interest and health. As this link between personal happiness and helping others gets more recognition and acceptance, it will be interesting to watch what direction this knowledge takes.

Perhaps taking care of our brother is the best way to take care of oneself? Isn't there a 'golden rule' about this?

## 93. The other day, some missionaries came to my door and were trying to convert me to their way of thinking. They were very insistent. Am I supposed to be open to this sort of thing or just ignore it?

A number of faiths have missionary work identified as an important aspect to their belief system. Wishing to share ideals that have provided much personal joy, believers wish to spread the good news and communicate this joy with as many people as possible.

In our own lives, we all have done some of this. Perhaps sharing good feelings about a new restaurant or television show, we encourage as many people as possible to join with us. Our enthusiasm is very contagious. So we all can understand the need and desire to share something of love and joy.

However in this situation we are discussing a personal belief system and may not wish to engage to the degree that the missionary, who knocks on our door, would like us too. Also in their zeal, the missionary may not be tuned to our need, and exert more pressure than we like.

If you encounter someone who wishes to sell something you are not buying and you request them to stop, however they persist, perhaps you need to try a more forceful approach. Do not worry so much about protecting their feelings.

Last, in this form of activity, i.e., missionary work, one must be careful not to create indebtedness or motivate through fear. Unfortunately this has not always been the case.

Historically some missionaries have combined necessities like food, clothing and shelter along with their work. Often it may be difficult for recipients to separate out the consequences of refusing a belief system and access to necessities.

## 94. Is there a faster way to do all this? Do I absolutely have to go through all these lifetimes to achieve the ultimate goal of spiritual studies?

There is a saying, among the Sufis, "what will take humanity hundreds of years to accomplish can be accomplished in one lifetime following the Sufi Way." This sounds very conceited, but from the Sufi perspective, this is a factual statement; it is not a boast, attempt to get new students, or an attempt to diminish the work of others. The Sufi Way, or following the inner teaching of all religious forms, is "the superhighway to God." According to the Sufi, other roads may get you there, but not as safely or expediently.

Historically scholars have identified the Sufi presence as a current within Islam; however true this observation may be, for there is indeed a Sufi presence within Islam, usually this observation is made by an outsider looking inward, who at best, partially understands what they are observing. Conversely scholars have asserted, a Sufi, or universal inner, mystical current, exists within all religious forms; this idea of inner connection, among all the religions, is also denied by just as many. To further confuse matters, some scholar's insist that Sufism lies entirely within Islam; and the presence of many Sufi Orders further confuses the spiritual traveler who wishes to understand this way of learning.

The reader is reminded, in order to understand a phenomenon; it must be viewed from the inside: within the form itself. To do this, you need first-hand information and experience. To this end, if you are truly interested in the Sufi Way, please refer to the body of work contributed by Idries Shah.

## 95. Do I really need a teacher? I like the idea of being my own guide. I'd like to find what interests me, study it and then move on. Can this work as an approach for me?

Much of our adult educational system is set up this way. If we have an interest in something, we sign up for a course and learn whatever is available. No longer interested, we move on to something else. In higher studies, students who act this way are sometimes called "spiritual tourists," and have signed up 'for the six countries in eight days package.'

In the realm of higher studies, certainly interest is very important. However other factors are more essential to the outcome. Do we have the temperament required? Can we learn from someone else? Is it the right time for this learning?

In every type of learning, there are preset conditions and the more advanced or complicated the learning, the more exacting the preset or entrance requirements. Imagine if we wanted to become a brain surgeon, we would have to undergo an extensive preparation, for years, until we actually met and worked with our teacher (brain surgeon). In this endeavor, the requirements are no less strenuous and we have to resist the urge to teach ourselves or prematurely 'operate on a brain;' someone may get injured.

## 96. All right, I understand all of this; there is a preparation that is required. However, I am impatient and want to get on with it. I wish to begin study with my teacher. What am I to do?

It is tradition that when a student presents him or herself to a teacher and is accepted before formal teaching begins, a period of waiting is prescribed. This is to test many things. Traditions vary and the length of time commonly used is 1001 days.

However, sometimes students are immediately accepted. Even with these students who are accepted without waiting, the proper 'level of sincerity' is recognized to be operating. This, the teacher assesses through spiritual perception and the teacher intuitively knows what each student needs.

In our society, it is very common to have spiritual learning courses offered like other academic subjects. All that is required to sign up is interest, time, and entrance fee. Some learning can be accomplished in this fashion.

However the learning we are describing operates differently. Many of the conditions under which it operates are very subtle and mysterious to most.

In the meantime, until it is the right time, the right

place and the right people are working together, remain optimistic. In this endeavor there are many things you cannot see and are hidden for good reason.

Who says that no spiritual learning is occurring? When you go to sleep at night, where does your consciousness go? It is said that at this time, the most spiritual learning takes place. Also, by the following the teachings of your faith, you are doing the work required for the next phase, whatever form that phase might take.

## 97. I have been accepted by a teacher and they have provided a course of study. It does not seem similar to what you are talking about at all! What do you say to that?

In this endeavor, we have free will and can pick and choose. As a caution, let me offer a few guidelines that are commonly accepted within genuine schools:

- In the course of study, has money passed hands? What is the expectation as to the form of payment that is required? In genuine schools, you are expected to make something of your life, not just a voluntary donation. Additionally, while money might be expected to further charitable works, money is not demanded, coerced or insisted upon.
- Has any fear or threat been used? For example, if you do not follow our way, you will suffer, not

reach enlightenment, and waste your time. Genuine schools encourage students to study whatever else is available and make their own comparisons. Usually, this is encouraged after some initial grounding, or study has occurred.
- In genuine schools, students are never asked to do things they are morally against. Students may be asked to study areas and take personal action that is uncomfortable at times, but these are never forced and evolve naturally. Within the school, sexual activity and using others for personal gain is forbidden.
- No prescription is made about withdrawing from the world. Genuine schools teach participation in the world (to make it a better place). If physical removal from the world is part of the training, it is usually temporary and for a limited period.
- There is no teacher worship. While the teacher is recognized to be special and gifted in many areas, the teacher's role is described as that of servant. The teacher's grace is recognized to come from a higher source, without which the teacher could not function.
- The outcome of the learning is a better person who more ably participates in the world. The teacher and student meet for a time and then the student is expected to move on with the rest of their life.
- The learning is recognized to be one aspect of what it takes to be a complete person; students are not expected to give-up autonomy and live apart from the world. They are to develop all of their talents and actively contribute to society

and improve the world.
- Both students and teacher do not do things that set them apart. They do not wear special clothing; they do their work as ordinary citizens of their culture. Their spiritual duties are in addition to their everyday role in society.
- The world is the school and classroom. Learning occurs on many levels.

Suppose your learning situation does not meet several of these criteria? You need to determine if your current experience is right for you and what needs are getting met; only you can make this judgment and take necessary action.

# 98. Within a spiritual context, it is possible to have two goals operating, when this carries to a third, something is lost. What does this mean?

Spiritual organizations, over a period of time, naturally expand their roles into social service activity. Some will add programs to enrich the mental health of families, others will raise funds to build a hospital, or expand into a larger building to become a much needed pre-school.

From a distance, when viewing these activities, each is an important contribution to the local community. However when the mission of a spiritual organization expands beyond a certain point, the primary focus begins to diffuse and even shift.

The primary goal of a spiritual school is to create an environment where completed men and women develop. This focus changes as the school begins to plan and deliver necessary social service programs. While it is possible to have some energy devoted to another area, this tendency has to be minimized.

For example, it is possible to offer opportunities for socialization and friendship within the context of a spiritual school. However this is not the primary reason for the school's existence and everyone should be clear about this. When this school takes on the responsibility of raising funds for a Friday Night Dance for teenagers, however important this might be resources of the school are used to run this activity.

The more this type of activity occurs, the more it is expected and as the focus shifts; eventually different types of people are attracted to the school.

# 99. Is there more than one name for God? Is it significant to use this name over another?

Tradition has it there are 99 Names of God and, as the 100$^{th}$ Name is Revealed, the individual receives great spiritual knowledge and responsibilities.

This is one of the many traditions of the mystical Path. God has Many Names and many Attributes; in speaking each Name or Attribute there is much Light. In fact many use the Holy Name for healing, prayer and focus in meditation.

Each of us has our own name and it is our individual designation, revealing much of who we are. In the world of spirit, each of the Holy Names, when spoken reverently is a vehicle to reach completion.

The 100$^{th}$ Name is hidden, and with it great power and responsibility are given. As God Wills, may your path lead to completion and the Holiest of Names revealed to you.

Until then, follow one of the great spiritual highways and seek the answer to the personal question: Who are you? And what did you come here to learn and accomplish?

May your journey be filled with Light.
-SB

# Part II

# Stories, Verses & Observations

# 100. The Theologian

There is a much repeated story about a Servant of God, and how he set aside traditional religious training to follow his mystical teacher and reach spiritual completion. And by under taking this journey, the world benefited.

One day, a Doctor of Theology was seated beside a water fountain, outside the university where he taught. Beside him on the fountain, were many books of religious law that had been passed down to him by his father, who in his time was a renowned theologian. As the doctor read through one of the books and memorized a passage, along came a desert wanderer. As was customary this fellow was dressed in a patched robe, with hair in disarray and a wild, far away look in his eye.

Before the Doctor of Theology fully noticed, the wanderer rushed forward and grabbed all of the doctor's books, including the one he was reading and tossed them into the water fountain.

Surprised and astonished at this behavior, the doctor called out, "Why did you do that? These books are filled with great wisdom and are priceless!"

The desert wanderer, stared at the doctor, then replied, "If you wish to learn something really useful; wisdom that is not found in your books then follow me." Then the wild desert wanderer turned and walked away.

Stunned and unable to move, the Doctor of Theology considered what to do.

Decidedly he left the books that had been passed down to him in the fountain and for three years followed this wild man of the desert. In time this doctor passed beyond knowledge of religion, into knowledge of self and spirit; becoming a sun whose rays still shine until this day. After their time together, nothing was ever heard again of the wild mystical teacher from the desert.

Today this Doctor of Theology, Jalaluddin Rumi, is widely recognized as one of the greatest mystical teachers and poets of all time.

# 101. Accepting God

>Why do people
>Have so much trouble accepting
>We came into this world
>To grow closer to God?
>
>While our time in this world
>Serves a multitude of purposes,
>In some respect, it will have been wasted
>Unless we come to understand and accept
>         this unifying principle.

# 102. The River

>*Traveler:* There is only One God, or Light,
>   Yet there are many paths and religions,
>   Why is this?
>
>*Master:*   Each traveler finds God / Light
>   In a different way.
>   One traveler may seek salvation
>   As a loving spouse and parent

And another may find God's Face
On a distant shore.

Each traveler is a universe
And in this vast expanse
It is easy to go astray.
Only the Light's Grace
Leads the traveler home.

Religion may be compared
To a great river that feeds the land.
The river winds its way as a mighty force
And smaller tributaries are formed
To serve the distant regions.
Some travelers are satisfied
To drink of the smaller stream
And forget they must travel
The river to its Source.

Beyond the river's gate,
The Ocean is waiting.

*Traveler:* Where is the boat
  To journey the river
  For I am ready to depart?

*Master:*  O little one, you are so eager;
  Yet you are already assail
  And your soul is the vessel.
  Your heart is the compass
  And the Light's Mercy
  Is the breeze at your back.

  If you bow in prayer to the Light,

The Light Will provide all you need
And Guide you to the Ocean.

## 103. Giant Bazaar

The world is a giant bazaar.
A market place
Where you will find
Exactly what you seek.

If you seek garbage, it is there.
Similarly if you desire sweets
There are many vendors.

Fortunate is the traveler
Who knows what to seek.
Most leave without making
The right choice.

## 104. The World

*Traveler:* What of the world?

*Master:*   All things in this universe
Are Created for an appointed term.
The sun, the moon,
And you and I
Are here for a brief afternoon
In the timeless eternity.

The Beloved is the Eternal Reality.
God was here

Before the sun and moon
And will be
Long after they are a memory.
This world is Created
For a fixed period
And when the hour arrives
It too will pass on.
Only God Remains.

*Traveler:* If this life is temporary
Why must I participate
In the every day affairs of the world?

*Master:*   Little one, you were Created
To serve God's Purpose.
Each traveler has a job to do
And each must contribute
To the benefit of all.
You will not serve the Creator
By sitting on a mountain
And praying for your own salvation.
We must participate in the world
And work for the benefit of all.

All of us cannot sit on mountains;
Who will do the work to feed humanity?
The secret is to remain separate,
Immersed in the Holy Name,
Yet participate in every day affairs.

Ask the Beloved
And God Will Teach you
The secrets of the world
And how to love His / Her service.

## 105. World as Canvas

> The canvas is the world.
> You are the artist.
>
> Pick up the brush;
> Create your own life.

## 106. Freedom To Choose

As spiritual travelers, we participate in the same design. We are born; we live and then die; traveling onto the next place. Yet within this pattern there is tremendous variability and much freedom to choose.

In the main how we live our lives is up to us.

## 107. Prayer

> *Traveler:* Holy One, speak to me of prayer.
>
> *Master:*   As the robin serenades the morning
> And offers thanks for another day,
> In this way, prayer is a song
> That arises from the heart.
> As the mother caresses the babe
> And her heart swells with love,
> In this way, prayer is sweeter
> Than the rarest wine.
>
> As the sun travels the heavens
> And heralds the morning,
> In this way, prayer is the work
> That we must do.

Prayer takes endless forms
And many times we are confined
To the ritual of praying.
True prayer is performing
All the tasks of the day as God's servant.

Remember we pray to the Beloved
Because we need God.
The Most High
Does not need our prayers.

## 108. Beyond Knowledge

Beyond words
And beyond experience
There is knowledge.

Beyond knowledge
There is God.
Here the seeker
And goal are united.

## 109. Be Not Shy

Beyond the mountains
God is waiting. Calling to the Heart
In sweet whispers.
Beckoning with a caress.
Come forward my lovers.
Be not shy of my Kiss.
Come forward and join me
In peaceful surrender.

Take one step toward me
And I shall fill you
With the Secrets of Eternity.
One tear from your heart
Longing for me
Shall lead you to the garden.
One sigh from your soul
Imploring my grace and mercy
Shall place you at my side.
One hand extended to another
In my Name
Shall raise the cup to your lips.

One life devoted to my service
Shall fill humanity with the rarest wine.

# 110. Bird Cage

Like a captive bird
The soul sings,
Remembering its home.

It is precisely
For this song,
The bird is caged.

# 111. Let Your Soul Soar

Chained to a world of illusion
Created by others and our desires;
How hollow are these dreams?

My soul cries out:
Fly away. Soar above these fences.
Go Higher. You are a Child of Light.

Rush toward the stars.
Go beyond the Sun.
There is your Home;
In the Nameless, timeless
Land that you have forgotten.

You are a Prince / Princess
And have come here
For a brief moment.
Let you soul soar, again,
Higher than the eagles,
Higher than the Angels.

You are the son / daughter of a King
And seek to embrace
All that is yours.
A timeless Spiritual Traveler
Who creates Reality
Upon Reality
All in the Name
Of that which is Greatest.
You are the door that blocks your way.
Open it.
Experience another part of yourself.

# 112. Higher Law

*Traveler:* Holy one, tell us of the Law.

*Master:* The Law is inscribed
On the heart of each traveler.
Beneath the layers of dust
That surround each heart is the Golden Rule.

The Law is also written in the Books
And is known to all.

It is written: *That which brings you closer*
*To the Beloved*
*Is the Measure.*

Travelers know what is holy and correct,
Yet allow themselves to be deceived
By their selfish desire.
If travelers would ask, in prayer,
God would help each traveler
Resist their own lower urges.

If you will pray and sincerely ask,
God will cleanse your heart;
And God's Law
Will light your inner darkness.

Remember if you will take 1 step toward
  God:
God will take 10 steps toward you.

## 113. Opposites

The sparrows play and flutter about in dirt.
Flapping their wings
They cleanse them selves with the soil.

If we did this
We would become dirty.
Requiring water to accomplish
The very same task,
We wonder how cleansing is possible?

Yet the same objective
May be reached by different means;
Sometimes they appear as opposites.

## 114. The Heart

*Traveler:* What of the Heart?

*Master:*   The Heart dwells
   Within the soul
   And is the window
   Through which we experience God.
   It is the fountain
   Through which the river flows
   And is the mirror
   Of God's Love.
   It is God's Gift
   To you and I.

   Some Hearts
   Easily perceive God's Wonder
   And others
   Are hardened to God's Glory.
   This mystery
   Is God's alone.

   The Heart

Is like the babe
Who yearns
To be in the mother's arms.
It is waiting to go home
And when God Calls
The rejoicing begins.

## 115. The Criteria

The inner wisdom or criteria has always been: *does the action bring you closer or distance you from your Beloved.* For your personal answer concerning each action and thought, learn to listen to your Heart and its own wisdom. Your Heart will help lead you Home.

## 116. Super Highway to God / Light

Each traveler must find their own wisdom, and will never be totally satisfied with the formulations of another. While a traveler can benefit greatly from a wise man / woman, ultimately each traveler must make their own way.

What a wise man / woman does is offer training, and is an exemplar, on how to unlock inner capacity to know. That is why there are so many books offering personal visions of wisdom; many travelers have found their own inner capacity and wish to share it. Yet what works for one will not work for another; hence the growing realization that self-help books usually fall short.

Ultimately, it is the grace of a Path and the traveler's own inner capacity that leads the traveler Home.

Waiting inside each is the Super Highway to God / Light; and precious are those who help a traveler unlock their own inner wisdom.

## 117. Raising a Candle

From time to time
I have to remember
Why I came here.
So often, the passing days
Cause me to forget.
You see, I hold in my hand
A candle, with a brilliant flame,
To fight the growing darkness.

Yet, when aglow
I raise my candle high
So others might see,
And the Light blinds them.
They run away, holding their eyes,
Shaking their head, confused.

So what am I to do?

Still, I raise my candle
Waiting for the weary traveler
Who needs a Light
To find their Way.
Then, as indicated,
I touch my candle to theirs
And together we travel
Illuminating the dark night.

## 118. Prayer for the New Age

Each is an eternal child of the universe;
A ray of Light from a larger, more glorious sun,
Traveling from world to world,
Creating their individual Reality.

O Radiances of Truth,
As this New Age Dawns
Fill us with joy and wonder.
Let your life giving energy
Rain down upon us;
Stilling all fear and worry,
Helping us to rise higher
Creating a New World
Of Light, health and beauty.

O Radiances of Truth,
May each heart embrace
Its own higher purpose.
Lifting their fellows;
Smiling, celebrating together
In the morning sun of Universal Love.

O Radiances of Truth,
May this New World start with me;
Bless my efforts to rise higher,
Every moment of every day,
And live according to my Higher Self
And the Higher Destiny of the Universe.

## 119. He Shall Walk

And he shall walk among us again.
His presence shall sing of breezes
From mountain streams;
Touching hearts with a loving caress.

All men and women shall bow before his
        majesty
And ask forgiveness for their fears.
He shall awaken a realization, never known,
Of the Creator's Mercy.

Men and women shall weep in the arms of
        their fellows.
Nations that were parted
Shall be joined
And all people shall again be One
With the Father / Mother.


## 120. The Prophecy

*Traveler:* Tell me of the Prophecy.

*Master:*   It is written
   That all you see
   Shall be destroyed
   And from the ashes
   He will arise.
   The Dove
   Shall be reborn.

   He shall spread his wings

    And gather together all of humanity,
    Drawing each person to God's Bosom.

*Traveler:* Why is this terrible destruction
    Necessary?

*Master:*   For many years
    Humanity has failed
    To follow the Laws
    And like the babe
    Who plays with the flame,
    The heat must be experienced.
    In the burning,
    The Lesson shall be taught.

    As the fire cleanses
    Our hearts shall herald
    The new world's birth.

*Traveler:* I am frightened.
    Tell me of the new world
    And ease my fears.

*Master:*   The mountains shall fall away,
    The night shall bow to the day,
    And each person shall awaken
    To the Name of God
    Caressing their lips.

    From the Dove's nest
    Humanity shall be joined
    In the One Religion.
    And each man will be cherished
    As part of the whole.

From the Creator's Heart
This wondrous dream
Shall become reality,
And you will experience it all.

## 121. Unseen Guardians

The balance between life and death
Is O so delicate:
A mere slip or twist while driving;
An electrical blackout;
An alteration in the balance of genes;
Each can result in death.

O spiritual traveler, why are you so haughty?

Do you really believe
You are master
Of your own fate?
Without the Guidance
Of the Unseen Ones
The flower of your life
Would wilt and decay.
They project the spiritual fabric
Which holds together this world.
Working in anonymity
They are the Selfless Ones.

## 122. The Designers

In every age and country
The Path has flourished.

It exists to make this planet
A better place,
And those who walk this Way
Are an enabling, creative force.
Their function is to provide
What is required
And unavailable from other sources.

Like the gardener who tends the plants;
Knowing when water, fertilizer or weeding
　　is required.
Always the action is in accord with the situation
And the Design that is emerging.

O you find this difficult to believe!
What matter if you believe or not?
This Reality exists
And without it
This world would cease to function.

Spiritual traveler, desist from the questions
That fill your mind
And listen to the answers
Which arise in your soul.

## 123. The Servants

*Traveler:* Who are the Servants?

*Master:*　They are those who seek God's service
And those whom God Selects.

Many are those who journey to God's Court
But only those God Caresses enter within.

Some were prophets,
Some were mothers,
Some were saints,
And some like you and I.

Each town and city
Has those who God Selects.
They are the greatest resource.

*Traveler:* What must one do
   To enlist in God's Service?

*Master:*   In the hearts of those God Chooses
   There is a burning to be with God.
   God Has Kissed their souls
   And Imprinted His / Her Name on their hearts.

   One day, because of a deed, or prayer,
   God Reveals His Face.
   Then the work begins
   And they strive to be accepted
   As a servant in God's Court.

*Traveler:* Will I be accepted?

*Master:*   Each person has their own destiny
   And serves the Creator's Purpose in a special way.

   If you seek God's Court
   Then pray and ask for God's Blessing.

Once you have started
The journey toward God
You can only gain.

## 124. Rare Jewels

The allegory of a treasure hunt or a search for a hidden secret is an old one. While no real treasure may exist, in terms of jewels or gold, there is indeed a hidden factor.

The capacity to perceive, or analyze every day events in a different way is the ancient treasure. Hidden within each of us is an 'organ,' which under the proper circumstance perceives the real patterns which shape our lives.

This capacity to see past the ordinary is our birthright and is taught to those who are fitted for it. The degree to which this capacity is awakened is in relation to the spiritual traveler's need in service to others.

It becomes operational only as it is used to help others and give people what they need, not what they think they need. This is how it works.

Service at its highest level occurs when we are able to look at ordinary events and turn them into jewels which really benefit others.

## 125. Higher Service

Duty is a task that you are expected to accomplish; it is a requirement of the situation and something which every one must do. If you are a baker, you must come to work on time, follow the recipes, produce the needed quantity of baked goods, and act responsibly to customers and coworkers. These are some of the general duties of a baker.

If these duties were to be totaled; this would constitute your service as a baker. Service is the compilation or total of a variety of duties and usually described in relation to other people. Therefore you bake bread, for example, for others to eat.

Service on another level relates to duties which are communicated and carried out on a spiritual plane. When one is in service to God / Light, the personal will is stilled and the servant acts in accord with the Master's Desire. Here the servant and Master are One, and the duties which are performed constitute the Higher Service.

# 126. The Exemplar

The Exemplar exists to show the traveler what is possible.

If you are lucky enough to find a wise man or woman don't be surprised if they don't dispense wisdom like a coca-cola machine. Wisdom is not the type of thing that can be offered to another person like an afternoon cup of coffee; it is a personal capacity that is developed over time, enriched by life experience and bestowed through spiritual Grace.

Also wisdom is individual and specific to time, place and people. So one person's wisdom or set of instructions and insights might mean nothing or seem like gibberish to another.

Even if a wise one wants to offer you some wisdom, often they are not able. The circumstances have not come together for this to occur.

This capacity to perceive subtle spiritual energy is termed attunement: the wise first show you how to find and listen to your own inner current; this is done by projecting Grace (Baraka) upon the traveler's heart and then sharing this Grace amongst travelers of the wise one's learning circle. During this energy exchange and spiritual preparation, individual exercises, prayers, readings and life assignments may also be given to help the traveler learn.

What you can receive from books written by the wise are exercises, preparations and words that inspire. These books may even lift you up and make your heart sing, but this wisdom is not your own song of knowing.

Above all, the wise are an example, a road sign to help you travel, develop along the Path and find your own way Home.

Wisdom is not fine words or advisory statements; wisdom is personal understanding and action which is in accord with the Divine Plan.

# 127. Raising Better People

> People treat others badly
> Because they do not know
> How to treat themselves well.
> The ills of the world
> Are correctable only
> By raising better people.
>
> Better people are produced
> Only through higher knowledge.

Higher knowledge is available
If you search for it
And are fitted to receive it.
That is the quandary.

The task of the rightly Guided Ones
Is to tend the flame of knowledge
And under the proper conditions share it.
These conditions include:
Right time, right place and right people.

So you think I am talking in riddles?
Perhaps I am or maybe
You need to change your way of thinking.

# 128. Choosing How to Live

Let me be perfectly clear: most if not all of the problems on this planet are caused by humanity and not caused by God / Light.

Presently this world is the way it is right now because people wish it to be this way; having set in motion natural laws which result in chaos, conflict, hunger and disease.

For a very long time now, humanity collectively has failed to acknowledge and live by the natural laws which govern our lives, physical planet and universe.

Too many voices have drowned out, with personal priorities, that each person has primary responsibility to self, family, community and larger world. Part of these responsibilities include: guarding and using our thoughts, globally sharing, protecting and helping one another.

As a species, long have we forgotten we are responsible for our thoughts, our actions, one another and our fellow living creatures. We have forgotten we are responsible for a Magic Wand: the thoughts we think and the actions we initiate physically and through our consciousness.

Let me ask you, why must one person have six houses and another go homeless? Why must one die from starvation while tons of foods are thrown out each day? Why must one go without treatment for disease while pharmaceutical corporations rake in billions? Why must one nation refuse to share its resources with another and threaten the world with nuclear disaster?

Yes, these are conscious choices made by people each day, all creating our collective reality. Remember our thoughts and energies govern and create a vast Kingdom.

For most people, what we think, create and do each moment and day is really up to us. How we choose to live our lives and influence others, our community and planet through our conscious thoughts and actions are all part of the responsibility of free will choice.

Creating reality is all part of the responsibility of living as a mature, human being.

## 129. Empty House

When the house is empty
And those we love have gone,
O how the heart cries out.

Yet on a deep inner level
We are never alone or very far apart.

For even at a distance
We have within a magical capacity
To touch those we love.
By concentrating and focusing
On the love we shared, in that moment,
We are again together.

Here in this place of celebration
There is no time or space
And we unite in each other's arms.

# 130. Parents

*Traveler:* Tell me of parents.

*Master:*  Your mother and father
Were joined so you might be
And from your mother's womb
You entered this world.

Most parents only desire
That which is best for you
And from a babe
They have watered you
With their love.

Thy mother and thy father
Are to be honored
And loved
For they are part of you.
Those who have mistreated others
And deliberately injure their kin,
Harm their own souls.

If you seek the Beloved's Court,
Only those who loved
And cherished all travelers
Shall enter within.

# 131. Spiritual Experience

I cannot give you
Spiritual experience;
This is something
This arises from within you
And is bestowed by the Unseen Forces.

Yet, I can remind you
That you must work
And strive
To seek the highest
In every action.

Then, as the Universe Wills
The flood gates shall open
And spiritual caresses
Shall flow outward
Like honey from the hive.

# 132. Searching for Truth

Once there was a man who traveled the highway in search of Truth. He stopped at every town and inquired. Sometimes the answers he received appeared to be useful and at other times, they did not. Always the advice he received was targeted at his worldly life:

get a job, marry and have children. Or don't work, live in a monastery and become a recluse.

Somehow these pieces of advice did not satisfy him so he kept searching. One day as luck would have it, he encountered a wise man who said, "The answer lies within." So for many years, this traveler with the help of the wise one examined the inner world and came to see these experiences as part of the answer he was searching for.

Slowly he realized what good is spiritual knowledge if it is not incorporated into the world? So he settled down, found a job, married and raised a family. As he worked, celebrated and worried, he came to see a truly spiritual life is a life that serves others and is guided by the Unseen Forces. And according to Design, he found real knowledge, used this knowledge in the way it was intended and the world about him benefited. All of this happened during the course of living day-to-day life.

# 133. Quiet Part of the Soul

Seek the quiet part of the soul. It is an island where you can rest and connect with what you need to know. All of this has been written many times before. It is nothing new. Perhaps, it is the first time for you; or for others a repetition of things you have heard before?

This quiet part of your soul knows. It is an organ of perception; something which has its own life. This aspect of the soul is able to perceive the hidden impulses which originate from the distant shore.

You are nothing more than a link in a chain which extends far into the past and reaches into the future.

What you can offer yourself and your children is an opportunity to drink of this wondrous heritage.

Work on yourself so you might become a channel through which this wisdom passes. It is within reach if you know how to grasp it. Come forward and claim your birthright. It is yours for the taking.

In the morning and evening, seek the quiet part of your soul. From there you may come forward, accept what is yours and live your dreams.

# 134. Spiritual Sight

That which is permanent is seldom known to the five senses. It must be perceived by another capacity. Until this capacity or organ of perception is awakened, we are like children playing with fire. Sooner or later our actions create problems for us.

The completed individual, or enlightened one, is able to temper their expectations with reality. Often it is our reaction to daily events and not the events themselves which pose the lasting problem.

We must learn to view and accept what is present; not what we want or expect to be present. By clouding reality with expectation and desire we shift off center. This lack of balance, in turn, prevents us from perceiving what is before us.

This capacity or necessary 'attitude' to view what is actually there may be learned. It is the birthright of humanity and is taught to those who are capable of using it in the proper way. By learning to view what is actually present, we are then able to perceive Higher or spiritual realities which manifest in this realm more clearly.

## 135. The Tapestry

*Traveler:* O Holy One, I have climbed the mountains and traveled the roads. I have made my way through wind, rain, sunshine and now snow to find you. Please tell me, in order to sit at your side, why must the road be so long and the journey so varied?

*Master:* Before I answer your question, first, you must answer one of mine. Do you agree to this arrangement?

*Traveler:* Hesitantly and with some annoyance in his voice, he replied, "yes."

*Master:* And from all this going and doing, what have you learned?

*Traveler:* After pausing and considering an answer, the tired traveler remembered one moment of clarity he had around an evening camp fire and offered-up this singular insight as answer. "Each day, while filled with a variety of disparate experience- looking back at day's end- they combine to make one journey…"

*Master:* "Now you are beginning to understand. Life, death, hardship, and joy are all part of the journey; combining to form the tapestry of life: from which you learn and move forward."

# 136. Spiritual Learning Outcomes

One of the many things the western spiritual seeker has to face is that within the context of our culture there is limited discussion and awareness concerning the outcome of spiritual learning. Also western spiritual travelers may have romantic ideas about what they will look like after they have reached 'spiritual completion,' i.e., added a measure of spiritual capacity. Often these expectations in part prevent the development that is actually possible.

Yet in other (eastern) cultures more familiar examples of the exemplar or 'wise one' exist; one who has balanced the self and added a degree of spiritual learning/capacity to their own daily consciousness; thereby helping self and others by tuning into something higher.

*Beginning Exploration*

In our culture, we have just begun serious discussion and exploration of the question: individually- what is the outcome of spiritual learning?

Often in the past, familiar examples of spiritually advanced travelers fell into the category of popular "Hollywood characterizations." For example, I remember my friends when we began our spiritual journey wondering, after we had suffered and purified ourselves, 'Will God talk to us and tell us how to part the Red Sea?' Or after we perform 3 miracles, will we be ready for sainthood?' Being unfamiliar with actual outcomes, often we made up jokes about all of this.

In our culture, the skills and capacities of 'wise one' have been transferred to a whole host of 'professionals.' We have guidance counselors, fortune tellers, therapists, life coaches, clergy, physicians, scientists and self-help books to tackle questions like: How do we reach human excellence? At what point do science, religion and medicine meet? Or how is spiritual development helpful in our highly complex daily life?

Fortunately for all of us the answer to these questions and methods to reach human excellence, through spiritual development, have been perfected already. Authentic traditions exist and slowly their hidden effect upon individuals is percolating its way into our mainstream culture and every day consciousness.

*Plan for Humanity*

These traditions assert: humanity, as a whole, has a cosmic mission / plan and over the ages is reaching higher. Within this Plan, it is each person's destiny to reach toward human excellence and become a more completed person. This development is accomplished one person at a time and includes the balancing of many skills and capacities. One of these skills being spiritual development; and in order for this development to mature, a period of spiritual learning must occur.

The outcome of this multi-faceted development: is a person who is equally concerned for their neighbor as they are for themselves and their family. Daily the completed person uses all of their abilities to make the world a better place, because they are attuned through spiritual development to the higher impulse. They go to work every day, raise their family and commute to work over crowded highways. They are part of the world, but have kept a part of them self detached and sacred. This aspect surrenders to the higher impulse, is part of their soul and helps integrate all of their capacities into our modern, hectic life.

*Individual Awakening*

In the 1950's these traditions began purposefully exerting their guiding influence upon our western culture. In order for these influences to mature and take hold, many things occurred and will need to occur. One of these being selected individual's awakening, understanding the outcome and potential of a more spiritual life and exerting their newly awakened influence upon their individual sphere of activity. In this way, the world will become a better place, one person at a time.

Today, this is a potential waiting to bud; both in our society and within the individual.

## 137. Book of Life

> The book of your life
> Has many blank pages.
>
> You are free to write on them
> Whatever you choose.

## 138. About Your Plan

> - Each spiritual traveler enters this world with a Life Plan or destiny. Often parts of this Plan are hidden and mysterious; yet the Plan exists and with a little guidance and concentration, aspects may be revealed.

- Some aspects and events in your Plan are fixed; however most of the Plan is totally up to you.
- Also each traveler enters with an individual, unique personality that has strengths and weaknesses; these personal characteristics help accomplish our Plan.

## 139. Surrender

*Traveler:* Speak to me of Surrender.

*Master:*   Herein is the Key
For all the creation
Bows to God's Will.

As God Wills
The moon gives way
To the morning
And the sun arises.
The galaxy dances
To God's Majestic Hand
And not a leaf falls
Without God's Knowledge.

The perfect servant
Is a slave
To the Will of God
And heeds God's Call.

*Traveler:* How does a person Surrender?

*Master:*   Surrender begins by realizing
Where we came from

And where we are going.
On many levels, this life is God's.

Only God can Teach
The depths of Surrender
And we must ask God
To show us the many levels.

## 140. Complicating Religion

Most travelers make religion too complicated a thing; adding rules and customs that many times get in the way of direct communication. Religion should be a joyous conversation between your self, your higher self and the Infinite. Religion should be natural; a joy and as refreshing as a clear, cool drink of water.

Travelers must learn to listen to the quiet stirrings of their heart. Here the communication is the sweetest.

## 141. A Guru

A guru is something or somebody from whom you have learnt something, not from whom you might or will, or whom you respect or whom other people respect. If you can't learn, the teacher, effectively, does not exist.[*]

---

[*]Idries Shah, Knowing How To Know, London: The Octagon Press, 1998, p.21

## 142. Signs of a Master

*According to the Risalat-i-Malamatiyya,* Bayazid was asked what would be the most important indication of a master who knew the secrets of the Sufi Way.

He answered:

"When he eats and drinks, buys and sells, and makes jokes with you, he whose heart is in the sacred domain- this is the greatest of signs of his being a Master."

Those people to whom you refer, who are devout, religious and absorbed, if they are incapable of detaching from these things- if, in fact these characteristics are obsessional- then they cannot be teachers of the Path.

This, in fact, is the chief difference between the indoctrinated person and the spiritual one, according to the Sufis.

It is indeed odd that this question still has to be asked today: over one thousand years after it was answered by Bayazid. This fact should make us realize how long it takes for knowledge to penetrate from being specifically targeted to being understood by people in general.*

## 143. Preparing For a Teacher

A question arises concerning what travelers can do or how they should occupy themselves while waiting for their teacher to call and begin formal study.

---

*Idries Shah, Knowing How To Know, London: The Octagon Press, 1998, p.228

- Examine personal assumptions about readiness for this type of learning.
- Develop 'sincerity' concerning motives and why one is interested in higher consciousness.
- Lead a balanced life. Fulfilling the minimum requirements necessary for the social structure in which you live.
- Consider that much of your responses to this learning are emotionally and excitement laden, and are the door which is in your way.
- Familiarize yourself with the body of work by a teacher; in preparatory materials, the entrance criteria will be specified.
- Associate with other travelers who have something to offer concerning the inner journey. Usually these travelers will present themselves as ordinary, not strange, and having adapted to their present culture. Typically being the type of person you would feel comfortable introducing to your mother and bringing home for dinner.
- Pray morning and evening to fulfill your higher destiny and the higher destiny of the universe.
- Remember in this endeavor it is a question of love. The lovers who wish to serve their Beloved are accepted. Love is never an easy path.

Finally, after considering this list of requirements, the traveler may become discouraged and wonder: is it worth the trouble? Surely, there must be an easier way? These requirements are just to get started. In this journey, it is a matter of burning. Those who reach journey's end are those who *have* to travel. For them, there is no other choice. They must reach the object of their love or perish.

## 144. Foundation of the Way

The Foundation of the Way, or Path, consists of 3 universal laws which take the form of actions and therefore have direction. These 3 laws constitute the framework upon which the Way is built and include.

1. There is a God / Absolute,

2. He / She Love His children,

3. And has created a Way (Path) for humanity to attain unto Him / Her.

While these 3 laws have their origin in Nature of God (Love), for purposes of this discussion, they are multi-directional. Laws 1, 2 and 3 originate in God and imply the action of God toward humanity, while Laws 2 and 3 imply reciprocity. It is by far the former set of actions (God to humanity) that are most important and eventually determine outcome.

If God / Absolute did not love His / Her children, then, God would not have created a Way for travelers to draw closer. Any progress along the Path begins with the realization there is a God who is the Ultimate Reality. This affirmation is the first step and for many the most difficult. It is so hard to believe and many never take this initial step. When the traveler spiritually realizes there is a God, who always was concerned, the traveler is in love, forever. God is the Beginning and End; and when the traveler embraces the Boundlessness of God's Love and Mercy the journey begins in earnest.

## 145. Path of the Spiritual Traveler

As previously indicated, most travelers make religion and spirituality too complicated of a thing. The following is the Path of the Spiritual Traveler in Every Day Life. Follow these 5 steps and you will travel beyond religion and spiritual Paths; embracing your own cosmic potential.

1. Love God / Light with all your heart and soul.

2. Be yourself and seek balance. Everything in moderation.

3. Make your life an hour of service and seek to submit to the Higher Call.

4. Pray morning and evening, giving thanks for this opportunity to help create your own life.

5. Help yourself and others reach higher. In each moment, choose the Higher Call. Give of yourself freely and help those who need a helping hand.

## 146. Awake & Manifest

For every traveler, one day this will all come to an end. It is as fleeting as a warm summer day. All that is lasting is God / Light.

Learn to awaken that which has been asleep, so in your present form, you may manifest your transcendent nature. That is the part which is lasting and will lead you into the next world. It is the part which will enable you to participate in the Plan and serve humanity.

Let it come forward; that is its destiny and your birthright.

## 147. Service

*Traveler:* Holy one, tell me of Service.

*Master:* As the stars in the heavens
  Give light to the darkness,
  As the sun gives warmth
  To the land,
  As the rain quiets
  The flowers thirst,
  So, it is with all God's Creation.
  Each is Created
  To do God's Work.

  Be like the river
  That waters the countryside
  And gives to all the people.
  Some will come to drink the water
  And others will come to leave their waste.
  Some will come to make their home
  And others will come to learn the Secrets.
  Like the river
  Let each take what he / she needs
  And flow onward.

*Traveler:* What is the nature of the Service
  That I must perform?

*Master:*   Each traveler is Created
  With many talents
  And the answer lies within.

  Ask God and God Will Guide
  You to your destiny.
  If you remember God's Name
  God Will Fill you with strength
  And your questions
  Will have answers.

# 148. Going Home

　　The acorn goes deep into the earth
　　And as the seasons pass,
　　Grows into a mighty oak.
　　Spreading its limbs for many years;
　　Giving shade and nourishment to the coun-
　　　　tryside.
　　One day, only to decay and return back to
　　　　the ground.

　　O spiritual traveler, when you close your
　　　　eyes
　　For the last time, where will you go?

　　The twin sparks of energy
　　That joined and exploded
　　Inside your mother's womb,
　　Carry you through your days.
　　Then one day this energy too
　　Must journey forward to someplace else.

Where will this energy take you?

Remember, it was Love
That brought you here,
And it is Love that will carry you
From world to world.

One day, to return Home.

# 149. Child of the Universe

Each of us
Is an eternal Child of the Universe.
Traveling from world to world
Living on
As Beings of conscious energy;
Creating one adventure after another.

In our present form
We are bound by physical laws.
When sickness and death enter
We forget for a time
Our individual greatness and invincibility.
Caught-up in the moment
Of pain and suffering.
Wondering why
It has to be this way?

O Child of Light
Remember this is but one port of call.
One stop of endless possibility
Along the glorious voyage Home.
Here we explore

The many aspects of Creation;
Learning, partners in the Divine Plan.

## 150. Be Yourself

Be who you are; seek to express yourself in the world and don't let others hold you back from your individual expression.

Often we are jailed by what society, friends, religion and family want for us. Sometimes this pressure to do something or make a specific life choice is with good intentions; other times it is simply a manipulation intended to hold us back or illicit a specific behavior.

Throughout your life, always, the prime directive: *be yourself* and if you have not spent enough time trying to figure this out- then today, that is what you are supposed to begin to do.

Find your own individual path and search your own inner knowing which allows you to do this. Because once you have figured out who you are and what you would like to do or be: the entire world, including you, shall benefit.

## 151. Learn About Yourself

Life is all about you; it is something you make up as you go along from moment to moment.

When you enter the earth phase, you bring with you certain skills, abilities and a life plan to follow. Always listen to yourself so you can hear what you would like to do.

Often the conditioning of society and its rules influences and disrupts what we would really like to do. Somehow you must go beyond this conditioning and find out who you really are.

Inside each of us, we have everything that we need to make the journey and must learn to awaken all the different parts of ourselves.

We are multi-level beings who have come here to experience, create and enjoy this opportunity to be who we really are.

# 152. Death's Call

Gently the ocean waves break;
As an old woman rests
Beneath the late afternoon sun.
Sitting in a worn beach chair,
Sheltered under her umbrella,
Listening to the ocean's soft lullaby;
Slowly she raises her head
And peacefully speaks across the water.

"You are nothing more
Than a warm afternoon in the sun;
An eternal vacation by the shore
And I am no longer afraid."

Very slowly, she rests her head
Back on her chest;
And for a moment, closes her eyes:
Breathing deep, the fresh ocean air.

## 153. The Change

*Traveler:* Why must we die?

*Master:*　In the living
　　Is the dying.
　　The nature of all existence
　　Is to change.
　　As the leaf falls from the tree
　　And gives life to the earth,
　　In this way, we must change to another form
　　To serve God's Purpose.

　　God Has Created us
　　To be here for a short time,
　　Then God Calls us to move on.

*Traveler:* During out time on this earth
　　What are we to do?

*Master:*　There are many mysteries
　　That we cannot penetrate
　　And many questions have no answers.
　　If the heart is tuned to the Creator in prayer,
　　Then the meaning to existence
　　May be experienced.

　　Before our birth
　　We were with God
　　And after our death
　　We shall return to God.
　　This life is to instruct us
　　In God's Service.

And in the world to come
We shall continue
To Sing God's Praise.

## 154. Ray of Light

When I am no longer here
I will have become
A ray of Light
Traveling through the air.
I will dance and sing
Before the smiling King / Queen.

My body will be no more
And through the galaxy I will soar.
A spirit of radiant love
That will glisten on the universal seas;
Reflecting God's Light for all eternity.

## 155. Serving Truth

Know we came into this world for a purpose:
To Sing God's Praise
And will leave it for another.
Find out what the relationship is:
For it will guide you in each realm.

Those who seek to serve Truth
And surrender to its manifestation
Have embraced Ultimate Reality
And need not worry about either world.

## 156. Love & Fear

> The easiest way to manipulate and control
> Is to activate our fear and reward mechanism.
> This built in protection
> Uses our main emotions: Love & Fear.
>
> O spiritual traveler, gaze about;
> See this manipulation in your everyday life.
> Identify its use
> So you might break free
> And rise higher than the angels.

## 157. Rebirth

Many are the mysteries and teachings about reincarnation; if travelers are reborn and come back for another adventure.

Yet, often forgotten are 2 important teachings: daily we awake from a small death, and each moment, we can start anew with another opportunity to create and destroy.

## 158. Morning Air

> It is time to go.
> The sun leads toward the west.
> Let us follow clothed in love.
>
> We go to a quiet, joyous place.
> Here you can wash your hair with sunlight
> And our spirits can live on morning air.

## 159. Giving

*Traveler:* Speak to me of giving.

*Master:*   We are brought closest
To the Creator
When we strive to be
Like the Most High.

Many were the sacrifices
Of the prophets of old;
Their love for God
Was their existence.

As the clouds give water
So the land might drink,
So the Creator
Showers His Love.

As the mother gives to the babe
In the Name of Love,
So the Creator Confers Grace
To all of humanity.

You must give and give
Until you are no more;
Then find yourself anew
In the Holy Name.

## 160. One Religion

*Traveler:* Speak to me of the great religions, and why each states their Path is the only way.  In the past religious difference has led to wars, killing and fighting. Why is this?

*Master:* On an inner level your religion is One Religion. Each religion is an aspect of the Divine. Just as clear light filters through a prism, changing, twisting to fit the demands of time and space; the colors of the prism are beautiful and varied; yet on inner level the light is without color.

The Inner Teaching is that the great religions are One; springing from the same Higher Source. Mankind has forgotten to sip of this ancient river and through the Light experience God's Love and Mercy.

One of the questions that reoccurs and is a point difficult to understand concerns God's apparent lack of interest in the world. The questioning mind wonders, why doesn't God do something about the world mess? People are so cruel to each other. Why doesn't God intervene and create heaven on earth?

There is a plan for humanity and it is evolutionary.

Over millennia, man is evolving to a higher spiritual condition. In time, people will become fully conscious of who they are and their own limitless inner potential.

The earth phase, or physical realm, is the classroom where this development and learning occurs. In order for progress to be accelerated, friction is required. This friction is by design and is an essential aspect of many lessons. It is this friction, pain and seemingly senseless destruction that people question. Yet all of this is part of the plan, until the collective learning is complete and humanity reaches higher.

Man is the creator of his own kingdom. For the most part, our consciousness and daily actions are freely chosen. In the morning, when we arise, we select many of the things we think about, eat and do. Collectively, when choices are for the higher good our race will have evolved to the next stage. Until this point, individually, it is our responsibility to become fully conscious of who we are and our limitless potential to create. Man is the microcosm and each is the Son / Daughter of a King.

## 161. Divine Friction

*Master:* Clapping his hands, the Master called to the Traveler, "Now awake from the slumber which has been your life and ask me the questions that fill your mind?"

*Traveler:* Slowly opening his eyes, trying to acclimate to the world of forms, the traveler queried, "Master, I know you have spoken about the meaning of opposites many times, and how on a deep, inner level they are really connected; combining to form the fabric of our lives. Yet, I am still confused; why must life be a series of ups and downs; happiness and sadness. Why can't life be a singular joyful experience of the Light? Why is the world created both as a source of great joy and sadness?"

*Master:* "The world is a multi-level expression of the Light; at their center, as you have just experienced, all things are connected and One; and once you have sipped of this Unity, your heart is joyful and triumphant — having tasted its home. Yet even with this proof, mind continues to question; for that is part of its job.

Remember, darkness and light; joy and pain work together by creating a friction or resistance, sometimes clashing in upon themselves; this resistance, or unease, propels the traveler forward; always seeking and questioning — until the day, when the traveler experiences the singular, connecting, glorious spiritual Unity and answer. As one of the Servants of God has said, "gazing at the earth from the moon, all things — human wants and desires — are lost in the Oneness of this magnificent, multi-colored orb as it travels through the heavens."

*Traveler:* And as the traveler sat and considered the Master's reply; he realized anew, in this journey, mind asks the question, and heart ultimately answers it.

# 162. Bending of Will

Following a spiritual path, early on, travelers are taught that life is up to them: we come into the earth phase with a multitude of talents, free will, a destiny or life plan and a wondrous world to express the many aspects of self.

Similarly, spiritual travelers are taught that higher levels of spiritual expression are achieved through submission; turning personal intention over to that which is highest both in themselves and the universe. Further in submission or giving up of self, which is not passive but active, the spiritual traveler finds completion and service. The great master or Sufi exists as an extension of the higher will; with each breath and action taken for the Beloved.

At first glance, personal action based upon free will

choice and submission to that which is highest appear directly opposite to each other. Yet for the spiritual traveler, there is a point at which these seemingly contradictory states merge; this coming together of personal will and submission to the higher is achieved through the alchemy of love.

Because we are in love, we wish to do what our Beloved wants. This fire of love, or burning, described by the mystic alters the consciousness: turning personal need into submission or bending of will; by practicing this bending of will, like the willow in the wind, the traveler becomes a stage upon which the Divine enters.

## 163. Prayer of Surrender

> As the willow bends to the wind
> And the leaf curls to the rain,
> O Lord, I surrender myself to You.

## 164. School & Learning

> Over the years I realized
> School and learning was not the same thing.
>
> While I grew to love learning
> Often school was dull and repetitious.
>
> School is a preparation for life.
> Learning is what life is about.

## 165. World as Classroom

The path exists to make better travelers who are more able to participate in the world. The point of spiritual studies is to add capacity and integrate other aspects of consciousness. This is done to raise the quality of every day interaction between people.

While a period of spiritual preparation apart from others might be required, and usually it is not, this separation is for a limited period. The learning is to occur in the world; this is our classroom and the spiritual traveler has multiple abilities that cannot mature unless they are exercised daily in the world.

If God wanted us to be solely of spirit and not participate in the physical, we would have remained in the spiritual realm. The body and our emotions are necessary to this part of the journey. Consciousness is a combination of physical, emotional, cognitive and spiritual stimuli; a balancing of these factors is required and is in part the goal of the spiritual journey. In order for each traveler to mature in their role as God's representative, all of these factors must reach full potential.

## 166. World Sickness

Humanity suffers from 'world sickness' and the teaching helps provide the cure and help the traveler see reality. Most people live their entire lives attached to ideas, possessions and different people. These things to the exclusion of others fill their consciousness. While it is good to be concerned about the things of the world and involved in making things betters for others, there is a point where this investment leads you away from the higher, lasting reality. A balance must be maintained between the physical and spiritual.

In this endeavor, it is a matter of degree and attitude. With the proper guidance the traveler learns to participate in the world and inwardly limit his attachment. While the traveler may go to work every day, work hard and try to help others, a part must remain 'sacred' and attached to the Light.

# 167. Inner Conflict

Sufis have long held that the inner war- Jihad, the fight between a traveler's higher and lower nature is a moment by moment struggle. Those who are somehow able to turn toward their higher self and use, in daily life, their access to spiritual awareness are on the road to enlightenment. This world is made a better place one person at a time and each person's life is made up of small moment by moment conflicts, decisions and actions.

Within each of us there is an ancient knowing and awareness that has been covered over by the dust of living in this world. This dust is comprised of things we are taught, things that we want and things that are necessary to living in the body. This friction between the things we want and need pushes us forward and gives life both meaning and urgency. Yet those who are able to overcome this pull and somehow elect things which help others have transcended the physical reality.

## 168. Reaching the First Stair

When you look around and consider those who have fallen or who are lost: have you ever wondered, what is the measure of their life? Yes, what is the worth of a lifetime that has been spent in darkness, straining, to reach the first stair?

We are not equipped to judge. The answer resides in boundless love: the Love of a Father / Mother who cherishes each the same; whether they are whole or lame; a Father / Mother who smiles equally at the slightest effort or the greatest gain.

## 169. Sunrise & Set

> When faced with the sunset
> It is easy to forget the morning.
>
> Yet both exist
> And follow each other.

## 170. The Heart Answers

For the spiritual traveler, life is filled with many experiences that cannot be answered by the everyday consciousness with a simple answer. Our mind balks at the senselessness of many life events; and it is only time, healing and the higher awareness of the heart; that eases the hurt and offers some level of healing.

Daily the mind reels at the destruction that seems to be intensifying around us and it is only time and distance that provide some sort of answer. Why does life have to be this way? Why do so many innocents have to die? That is something that only your heart's inner wisdom and God's Mercy can answer. It is an answer that must be experienced, emotionally and spiritually.

Know that the answer is found in Love; as the poet Attar states: *The whole world is a marketplace for Love.* This includes the good, bad and seemingly senseless destruction all about us.

Without the friction and pain of daily life, who would turn toward something Higher and embrace the potential of another form of existence?

## 171. Evening Fire

> When like the smoke
> From the evening's fire
> We have faded into the night;
> It will only be God's Love
> That will Guide us Home.

## 172. Faith & Knowing

> *Traveler:* Holy One, I am afraid.
>   Teach me to quiet my uneasiness.
>
> *Master:*  Little one, man / woman has always
>             trembled
>   In the darkness
>   And reached out for help
>   In his hour of need.
>   We were created with limitations
>   And our vulnerability
>   Leads us toward God.

As the sunlight quiets the darkness
Faith in God quiets all fears.
The Light in the darkness
Is the Holy Name.

*Traveler:* Please tell me more of faith and knowing.

*Master:* Faith is understanding
That God Guides us
And realizing God will always be.
Faith is knowing
That in each event God is present
With our best interest closest to His Heart.

Faith is a cornerstone of life
And is the foundation of the Temple.
Faith and knowledge is the rarest of jewels
And when God Wills the treasury opens.

# 173. Knowing

Most spiritual training programs teach the traveler to pray or turn inward in some fashion before making an important decision or taking an important action. Within each person, there is an inner voice or capacity to know if an action will bring us closer to our higher self and the higher destiny of the universe. Most people have forgotten to develop and listen to their own inner voice and have relied upon others to teach them about right and wrong.

This original social, moral and religious teaching about what is useful in life, was intended as a beginning; and the traveler, as they matured, was to be instructed on how to make their own more complex, intuitive decisions. For many, this has been omitted from their training and they continue to rely upon limited and simplistic learning constructs.

## 174. Physical Form

>Of necessity that which originates
>In another realm
>Must undergo change
>To manifest in this one.
>
>That which is formless
>Takes on a physical shape,
>So, we may know it.

## 175. Origins of Wisdom

Sometimes I wish I had something profound to say: words of wisdom that would echo through your soul and remind you of your Divine Origin.

Yet wisdom is not like this... it must be earned through life's ups and downs. Also it must be something the seeker experiences him self and strikes a chord deep within his soul.

In every cell of their body, most spiritual travelers forget they have all the accumulated wisdom of the ages. All they must do to access this Treasure is to Remember and go inward; and for most travelers it is life's friction that turns them inward: searching for an explanation, healing or an answer to a series of troubling events.

You ask: what is this process to Remember and go inward? It is not as difficult as you think. You remember by following a Path to spiritual completion. Further you wonder: how and where do I find such a Path? The offer is right before you: look closer- it is there.

## 176. Talking to God / Light

When traveling the mystical path, travelers often want prayers, exercises and techniques that will work for them. We request guidance from one who has traveled a little further or even reached their goal, hoping that with practice, these techniques and exercises will increase our understanding and proximity.

Often what is missing from this selective use of other travelers' practice is that each traveler's position along the path is different; and what worked for one will not automatically work for another. Not factored into the learning structure are determinants such as readiness and Grace.

Let me share with you an ancient technique that is guaranteed to work and help you move closer to your goal. Direct communication or talking with God / Light is absolutely guaranteed to help you move further along your path. Each morning and evening, and throughout your day talk to God / Light; cry to God / Light; and ask for whatever you need; and seek to make yourself a channel through which this communication continually flows.

Daily, talking and Being One with God / Light is guaranteed to open your window of knowledge and understanding.

Further, just as the young babe coos in their crib or the maple stretches it branches out to the sun; this talking and direct communication with the Light should be as natural as breathing.

Yes, touching God or the Infinite is as simple as calling out the Name of Your Beloved, over and over again.

## 177. Greater Freedom

Looking back, so much of my life has been spent seeking things I thought were important. In fact, most of my waking hours have been spent in this pursuit.

Through the Mercy of the Path, there comes a time when I put aside my desires. It is in these moments that I am most free. A heavy weight is lifted from my shoulders and I experience True Reality. I am free to do or not do, depending upon the Design before me. Because I am no longer concerned about my needs and focus on the present, I drink of a greater freedom.

## 178. Hand of Fate

Two young worms were crawling about the worm farm discussing their bright futures. The first, who was the larger of the 2 boasted, "Someday I am going to be the King of all the worms. I will win the honor by defeating all you smaller worms. Then everyone will know my name and come to me for advice and help."

The second worm that was also large for his age was not as ambitious as the first, but he too had dreams of the future; and added, "Someday I would like to be able to say I climbed every hill and traveled each tunnel in this land. I will have seen everything there is to see and everyone also will know my name."

Then the first worm replied, "O our futures look so promising. Perhaps I will even make you the official explorer to my court."

As the 2 worms basked joyfully in their plans for the future; the farmer's hand descended into the farm and scooped them both up.

*The Lesson*

- While it is good to have plans for the future and something to work toward; these plans must be aligned with your potential or design of the situation.
- Yes in order to attain our goals: everyone must have talent, hope, plan and work hard. However, keep in mind, there may be other factors at play.
- Fate and the Unseen Forces / Absolute may have something different to say about our future.

# 179. Inner Walls

Each of us builds walls
To hide away our fears.
Our daily patterns of work and play
Can be jailors which bind
Our true, lasting nature.

Of what are we afraid?

O fragile one,
We are the caterpillar
Who is too timid
To break out of the cocoon.

## 180. Process of Change

Just as water must undergo change
To become ice and snow,
So must we undergo
A process of alteration.

Slowly the world of the senses
Must be taught to give way
To the world of the soul,
Then the change is complete.

## 181. Always Getting What You Want

Consider the possibility that people are always getting exactly what they want by creating problems for themselves so they will have something to do, keep themselves busy and continue to struggle; this creation of personal problems confirms their inner world view: the world is a harsh place and full of pain. Often this mechanism is operating on what we call a subconscious level and people are not fully aware, most often, they are the source of their own problems. And while the worldly consciousness is occupied with these daily concerns, creating and solving persistent problems, their higher consciousness lays dormant.

In order for the higher consciousness to operate and be maximized, the worldly consciousness must be stilled and pushed aside for a time. This is an essential aspect of the inner journey; time to be still and hear the inner call. Practice this exercise daily, and as God / Light Wills, one day you will awaken to find this higher mode of thought is as natural as the other.

Do not be afraid! You are the door which stands in your way. Learn to recognize your own inner road blocks. Go beyond fear and learn to operate on another level; here you will find peace and awareness in the Ocean of the Beloved's Love.

# 182. What If

    What if all the money, energy, thought and time
    Used for war and countries fighting each other
    Was used to feed the hungry, care for the sick
    And help those in dire need?

    Yes, what if all across the world
    Soldiers, sailors and flyers
    Turned their attention and energy
    To healing and building
    Instead of defending and fighting?
    And what if, in every land,
    The manufacturers of guns and weapons

Used their resources to build homes for the homeless
And hospitals for the sick and dying?

Can you imagine such a world?

That's the world we should be reaching to manifest.
Ask any soldier which is a better choice- life or death;
Yet many are not ready to abandon their old ways.
This way of killing and fear serves individual purpose.

How long will it take for humanity to learn the lesson?
The choice to build or destroy
Is ours, collectively,
Every moment of every day.

# 183. To Be

So you think you will be successful on the Path.
Have you ever considered the source of your belief?

Perhaps you are mistaken
And this idea is just another form of greed.
Or you might really have the capacity
And it is just a matter of time and training.

Foolish one, give-up your circular arguments!
These thoughts and questions were designed
To take you part of the way,
Then the ego must die.
Switch to another mode of consciousness:
And Be
That which you were created:
To Be.

## 184. The Books

*Traveler*: If the heart is the key
  By which we realize God
  Then why were the Books written?

*Master*:   The Books were Sent
  As a Gift for humanity.
  The words are notes
  To serenade the heart
  And each phrase
  Sings God's praise.

  The Creator planted a seed
  And it grew into a mighty forest.
  God Kissed a child
  And she blossomed into a flower.

  Herein is a Code
  For humanity to follow.
  Each Book proclaims God's Mercy
  And clearly explains the Law.

*Traveler*: With the Law clearly written,

Why have so many gone astray?

*Master:*   The heart is a traveler
  Of many journeys
  And each trail
  Is filled with danger.

  Some travelers are forever lost
  In the beauty of the rolling hills
  And it is only God's Grace
  That allows the traveler
  A safe crossing.

  The Books are a sign-post
  To help Guide the Way.

# 185. Bottled Water

While grocery shopping, have you considered how many brands and the variety of bottled water available? There is natural, cold spring, hot spring, sport, vitamin enhanced and countless diet and non-diet carbonated soda water.

Also, at meals, have you noticed how rarely water is the beverage of choice? In some restaurants, you have to ask for water before they will serve it; and it is not uncommon for some children, in their own home, to go days without a plain, glass of water.

It is the same with humanity's religion. There is an endless variety of forms, and for most people, the 'water' must be sweetened and dressed-up before they will drink it.

## 186. Higher Reality

> Beyond words and desires there is an underlying Reality
> That unifies all things.
> This Reality and the method to perceive it
> Is the birthright of humanity.
>
> In their journey through this world,
> Most travelers become distracted
> And fixate on all manner of things.
> In a sense these things become their reality
> And then have no need of anything higher.

## 187. Time Dragging On

> Brief is our stay in this world.
> Yet as we disconnect
> From our higher nature,
> These hours seem like an eternity.

## 188. Be a Beetle

A beetle was buried beneath a ton of earth and began to scream, "Help me! Help me! I am buried alive. Surely I am going to die."

After sobbing for hours, suddenly the beetle realized he wasn't dead. Then, it occurred to him he was a beetle and beetles were supposed to be in the ground.

Later, after further thought, he began climbing through the earth, toward the daylight and other adventures.

*The Lesson*

- For the spiritual traveler, there is a period of inner search and turmoil.
- Then one day, we remember and realize, that we are also of spirit and begin reaching upward toward our lasting lives.

# 189. When You Are Flying

A young sparrow was complaining to her mother, "You are always showing me how to fly. You have shown me all your techniques and regularly discussed the various principles involved, but when will I actually take off and fly? I am tired of practicing and preparing. When will I fly?"

In an even tone the mother replied, "When you are ready."

"How will I know when I am ready?" continued the youngster.

"When you are flying," replied the mother.

*The Lesson*

- The inner awareness, once awakened, is as natural as breathing. Or in the case of the young sparrow: as natural as flying.
- The question you should be asking, " Is how do I awaken this capacity? What preparations do I need to make?"
- In part, that is the role of the mother / teacher; to assist in this preparation.

## 190. Enlightenment

Learn to see those things
Which you must do
And those things
Which God / Light must do.
He / she who can recognize the difference
Is on their way to enlightenment.

Most travelers expect enlightenment
To arrive in a flash.
They imagine it is like turning on
A lamp in their home.
This is our desire for haste
And stems from greed.

This process is much slower
And knowledge comes in stages;
And once the Light is on
It cannot be turned off
As easily as hitting a switch.

## 191. Judgment Day Song

And on the Judgment Day
He / She shall Command:
>     Recount to me
>     The good and evil
>     That you have done.

And we shall be called
To answer for our deeds.
Each part of our body

Will receive a Command:
> *Lips.* Tell me
> Those you have hurt.
> *Arms.* Speak to me
> Of those you loved.
> *Feet.* Number those
> You walked past
> And did not help.
> *Heart.* Sing to me
> Of the joy
> You brought to others.

And so it will be
With each limb.
And so it must be
With each soul.

## 192. Higher Forms

The Sufis assert that the highest form of service is selfless, anonymous service that is aligned with Truth.

Ordinary charity, or giving to others, is part of being a human being. It is something which is expected in everyday life; it is part of the basic requirement of responsibility towards others. Further, in order for helping to be most effective, it should be done in secret.

In our society, most often, we make a display of generosity. Pictures which are donated to hospitals have a plaque with the donor's name on it. Or lists of donors to a charity are published in newspapers.

This is a beginning and important, however, other levels of charity and giving exist. When the recipient knows the giver's identity, there is a risk of obligation.

Giving, which is free of obligation or a feeling of reward should be the goal. Giving must be out of the necessity of the situation.

## 193. What is Sufism?

*Traveler:* When friends ask me what I study, and I try to explain, I find it hard to put into words, what is Sufism? Help me understand so I can give a clearer answer?

*Master:*   One of the great teachers offered, 'long before there was a name (Sufism) there was a reality. Now there is a name without a reality.' What is meant by this is that there has always been a way to connect with and experience ultimate Truth; this spiritual path of learning existed long before travelers, in the late 1800's, gave this way of learning its present name- Sufism. At the time, local ascetics wore a distinctive woolen (Soof) robe and became known for this. Now this name, or spiritual form, for many followers exists without a corresponding inner reality. Often today, what you see in the world represented as Sufism is an empty shell of its former self.

   This ancient Path of spiritual development is based upon connection with and experience of the Divine. It involves study with a teacher and the awakening, through direct contact with Truth, of latent spiritual capacity; this is done so the traveler can help others. This Truth or universal essence, is the underlying energy or fabric of created forms.

   This Path existed long before there were religions; this way of learning is at the heart of the great religions; it is the underlying spiritual energy that gives everything in the universe its form and substance. Inside each of us is an aspect of this wondrous element. Through preparation, practice developing our inner spiritual awareness, and Grace we unite with and serve Ultimate Reality every day.

My teacher called this Path: the Superhighway to God. For those who wish to connect with Truth and use their inner spiritual capacity to help others; this form of learning is available in every town and city. Sufism is not something talked about or described in written words; it is a universal essence that is experienced and known through inner spiritual contact. Much like love; no matter how many words you use: the description is not the same as the actual experience. And like love which ebbs and flows, Sufism changes to fit the learner, time and place.

*Traveler:* This helps a little. Sufism is difficult to put into words because it is a spiritual experience and changes with each person. Yet, I have been in love and know there are different forms of love with many peaks and valleys that are impossible to describe; and no matter how pretty a poem or love song, it is not the experience itself.

*Master:* Remember, everyone is a spiritual traveler and in their long journey through this universe, experiences many wondrous things. Countless experiences go beyond words and cannot be written down: changing with each moment and person. This dimension is one of the elements that make life multi-level and beautiful. If this is too difficult for those who ask about us to grasp, ask them to define love or even life itself. As they ponder all the possibilities, then, they will begin to understand.

# 194. The Teaching

The questions were completed
And God's Kindness
Brought tears from the Heart.
Then the Master spoke
About the miracle that had occurred.

*All of the concerns
That were in your hearts
Have now been Answered.
The uneasiness has been quieted
By God's Loving Hand
And the Beloved Has Filled us
With His / Her Grace & Mercy.*

*As you leave this book
And journey out into the world,
Remember, all your questions
Shall be answered by faith.
When your heart calls
The Holy Name,
All that will matter
Is the Beloved's Caress.
His Name shall be your Home,
Herein is the Teaching.*

# 195. The Prince

In an age long ago, there lived a handsome Prince who was beloved for his joy, kindness and generosity of spirit. The Prince's father, the King, recognized that his son was very special and did not want him embittered and tarnished by the world. So, the King built a high wall around the palace and kept all knowledge of the darkness and despair of the world away from his son. In the presence of the Prince, none were allowed to speak of sickness, war, poverty or the world beyond the Palace. In this way, the King kept his son sheltered from the ills and sadness beyond the Palace walls.

As the years passed, the Prince married and had a family of his own. While his life in the court and family activities kept him occupied and for the most part content, the Prince was beginning to feel a faint stirring within his breast that he could not identify and this caused him concern. When he spoke to his wife, the Princess about it, she told him, what she had been instructed to say by the King; it was a feeling that would pass and not to be concerned.

As this feeling of uneasiness did not leave, one day, he went to his father the King, to see what could be learned. The Prince questioned, "Father there is restlessness inside my heart that is causing me concern. While my life in the Palace is full, I am beginning to wonder if I am missing something? I know there is another world outside the Palace; I have heard people at court whispering about it. I would like to see and learn of this world."

The King replied, "yes my son, there is a world beyond the Palace, but it is nothing as beautiful or grand as our life here at Court; in the outside world, there are things like poverty, war and hunger. Also, there is an emotion called pain that is very unpleasant. That is why I have built this wall and, all these years, kept these things from you."

And the Prince, because he had an inner sense of wisdom, replied, "thank you father for protecting and being honest with me; however, the outside world is something I will need to think more about."

As the Prince left the court, the King who was very wise, assigned two Palace Guards to watch his son and make sure he did not go exploring into the outside world.

That evening, as everyone slept, the Prince changed into some old clothing that he purchased from one of the stable hands and climbed out a window in a quiet part of the Palace, where few people slept, carefully avoiding the guards. He made his way to the Palace wall and climbed over with rope and grappling hook; the stable hand had concealed earlier in the day.

And as the Prince climbed the wall, in short time, he found his way to the village that lay a distance over the hills. Walking through the village, as people prepared to bed for the evening, the Prince saw people, without homes, living on the streets that came-up to him, begging for food. And as he walked, he saw a man without legs that worked selling cooked meats beside another, missing one eye, who was cleaning potatoes to bring home to his family.

All the while, the Prince walked among the villagers, they did not recognize him. For the Prince was dressed like one of them and was no longer joyful; his gait was bent like one who struggled with a heavy load. And indeed this was true; the poverty, illness, and sadness about him had burdened the Prince and caused him to despair.

That night the Prince did not return to the Palace; he spent the hours walking across the countryside unable to reconcile the gaiety of Palace life and the seeming poverty and suffering of the nearby villagers. Why hadn't the King, or any of his Advisors, done anything to help these unfortunates? The Prince knew that his father, the King, was a generous man; over the years, the King had refused the Prince nothing as he grew into manhood.

Yet, the King surely knew about the situation? The village was so close to the Palace. Finally, the Prince reasoned, the King allowed this poverty and by contrast, the extravagance of Court life. This troubled the Prince further.

And as the Prince continued to walk, the sun was coming up as he approached the plain before the great forest. In an open grassy space, the Prince saw some poorly dressed men gathered in a circle, seated in lotus position. Coming up to them, he called out, "O men of the forest, may I join you and learn something of your way of life."

And the oldest of the forest hermits, who introduced himself as Jedaya said, "you may join us if you are not faint of heart and firm in resolve. We live a lonely and poor life. Often we sleep beneath the stars with no roof over our head and no bread in our belly. What say you?"

And the Prince, who made up a name for himself, replied "greetings Jedaya; my name is Sadhru and I am firm of resolve. I wish to join you only if peace can be found in your way of life. What say you to this?"

"Sadhru," replied Jedaya, "it is said that peace may be found in the hermit's way of life. Do you wish to join us?"

For ten years, Sadhru joined the forest hermits and lived among them, studying their ways. In this period he learned many things. Sadhru learned to recognize the coming storm by the song the leaves sang in the wind. He learned which berries were poisonous and how to fashion a loincloth from among the reeds. He learned to quiet his heartbeat to a gentle stir. Yet, in this time he did not learn to rise above, or still, the pain in his heart caused by the suffering of the villagers and shame of the King's indifference.

One morning as the forest hermits sat in their meditation circle, Sadhru informed Jedaya, it was time for him to leave. Sadhru indicated, he had learned many things, but had not learned to still the pain in his heart, and this pain was forcing him to find another way, a way to transcend pain and suffering. And Jedaya was sad to see Sadhru leave and looked upon Sadhru as a son.

And as Sadhru traveled for days, further into the forest, he came to rest beside a peaceful river. Here he slept and refreshed himself; and while he slept, he dreamt of a grass hut, beside this river. In this hut, he saw himself and another, older man; they both worked together, happily as ferrymen, taking people by raft across the river.

When Sadhru, awoke from his dream, he was cheerful for the first time in over ten years. This happiness filled him with energy and he quickly resolved to locate the ferryman and make this dream a reality. In his time with the forest hermits, Sadhru learned to read the signs of the forest, lake and stream. By intuition he could tell that the river was flowing faster up ahead which meant that it was growing wider, downstream.

This was the direction that Sadhru followed.

By early morning, he saw the hut, the ferryman and people being transported across the river just like in his dream. As the ferryman docked and tied up his raft, Sadhru offered assistance and worked alongside with the ferryman for the rest of the day. At day's end, as was the custom of this land, the ferryman invited Sadhru to rest and partake of tea and melon. And as the two men sat together and sipped tea, a friendship was instantly formed; and Veda, which was the ferryman's name, asked Sadhru to join him with his work.

Sadhru agreed, "only if I can find peace, and transcend my pain and suffering working on the river." Veda softly replied, "I have worked on this river for 30 years and have found peace and bathed in the still water of my soul. Here, in time, you will find what you are seeking."

And as the years passed, Sadhru learned to hear the beautiful song of the river. It played a quiet, peaceful tune in the winter and in the spring rejoiced in its new life and wonder.

When people came to cross the river, they remarked how similar both the ferrymen appeared. They looked like brothers, and emanated a quiet, joyful, peace about them.

One sunny afternoon, Sadhru rested beneath the trees that lined the river. And as Sadhru sat and mediated, in lotus position, Sadhru began to hear a faint melody stir from deep within his breast. Slowly Sadhru recognized the song; it was the same joyful melody the river sang as it celebrated its new life and carried the melting snows.

And as Sadhru merged with his own inner song, he rejoiced in its peaceful beauty, and joined with the notes of the river. Like two lovers surrendering to each other, Sadhru and the river became one. In that serene moment that carried into eternity, Sadhru celebrated and journeyed with the river across the countryside; and as the river fed the land, Sadhru joined along with the fields and trees as they drank of the cool, peaceful water.

In that moment that stretched far back into the past and far into the future, Sadhru was one with all living things; finally, he was at peace and had transcended his own pain and suffering.

In the years that followed, many came to learn beside the ferrymen; in time, this way helped many transcend sorrow and cross the river of life. First, they had to leave their old ways behind and let the ferrymen guide them.

# Epilogue: A Call to Hearts

When are we going to stop thinking in terms of religion, country, tribe, town, neighborhood, planet, business and I. When will we begin to think in terms of humanity and helping all people reach higher? Yes. It is natural to think about self, but when are we going to start thinking about and helping others? Feeding the hungry; giving care to the sick and dying; helping the young child to fight hopelessness; learning to use their abilities to help self and others.

Yes. We are all creatures of selfishness and selflessness. Again I ask: when will the day arrive when we think of our neighbor as our self and not compare what he / she is earning and consuming. Through electronic media, we live in open age where we can discuss our baseness and talk about the glory of rising above this lower nature; helping our fallen friends.

Again I ask: when will the day arrive when we actually do something to lift ourselves higher and in this process of reaching higher, lift our neighbor along with us?

It is only fear and a dark heart that stands in our way. We have before us unprecedented capacity to communicate with each other. This communication is provided through the internet, television and social media. When will all the people of this planet call out to each other and join hands; connecting hearts to make this is a kinder, more humane planet?

Remember. It starts with you and me. Each day ask yourself: what did you do to help yourself rise higher and what did you do to feed the hungry or bring a smile to a suffering friend's face? Stop thinking in terms of my religion, my job, my world and my planet. Start thinking in terms of higher self and how we can help humanity reach higher.

Personal maturity arrives when we stop thinking so much about self and think and act for others. Too long through religion, country, town, business we have been taught to think of self and how we can personally benefit; now it is time to think of others and reach out across this planet so we all may benefit.

This is a call to hearts- a call to each heart that wishes to help their fallen brother / sister.

O children of flesh rise higher and embrace the glory of helping others; so people will no longer go hungry, sick and be without home or without hope.

O children of tomorrow follow your heart; reach out each day and help yourself and someone else reach higher. Remember, this change starts with you and me.

# Books By Stewart Bitkoff

- Journey of Light: Trilogy, Authorhouse, 2004.
- A Commuter's Guide to Enlightenment, Llewellyn, 2008.
- Sufism for Western Seekers, Abandoned Ladder, 2011.
- The Ferryman's Dream, Abandoned Ladder, 2012.

To contact author go to: www.stewartbitkoff.com

www.ingramcontent.com/pod-product-compliance
Lightning Source LLC
Chambersburg PA
CBHW051752040426
42446CB00007B/322